MW01178721

I Lost My Breast and Found My Soul

Joanne (Sheppard) Rybar

VANTAGE PRESS
New York

Cover design by Susan Thomas

FIRST EDITION

Copyright © 2004 by Joanne (Sheppard) Rybar

Published by Vantage Press, Inc.
419 Park Ave. South, New York, NY 10016

Manufactured in the United States of America
ISBN: 0-533-14657-7

Library of Congress Catalog Card No.: 2003094053

0 9 8 7 6 5 4 3 2 1

This book is dedicated to
Katie Alfs—a special therapist
and
Is written in honor of St. Anthony

Katie, I thank you for
Your spirit of love and caring,
As you continue your work
To help others find
and
Awaken their spirit of love from within.

St. Anthony's of Padua—
If there is honor to be received
From these writings,
All praise belongs to you.

Thoughts for the Day—to Help Us *Through* the Day

<u>Change Your Life</u>
Tell the truth.
Face life openly.
Say what you mean, feel, believe.
Accept yourself as you are.
Accept others as they are.
Know and accept your weaknesses.
Stop trying to prove yourself.
Let go of the past.
Give up false expectations.
Take responsibility for your life and how it turned out.
—David Viscott

The thing that is really hard, really amazing, is giving up on being perfect and beginning the work of becoming yourself.
—Anna Quindlen

"Lord, what are you up to today?—I want to be a part of it. Thank you." Amen.

—Crystal Cathedral

The longer we carry a grudge, the heavier it becomes.
—Anonymous

In the attitude of silence, the soul finds its path in a clearer light and what is elusive and deceptive resolves itself into crystal clearness. Our life is a long and arduous quest after truth.

—Mahatma Gandhi

He had occasional flashes of silence that made his conversation perfectly delightful.

—Sydney Smith

Call to me and I will answer you, and will tell you great and hidden things that you have not known.

—Jeremiah 33:3

The unspoken word never does harm.

—Kossuth

I have heard your prayer; I have seen your tears. Indeed, I will heal you.

—2 Kings 20:5

Contents

Author's Note

My Thank You

I would like to thank my <u>Husband</u> who has always encouraged me to write. Ron has never voiced a complaint, concerning the time I spend writing and bringing my book to completion. He just seems to know what it takes. He displays to everyone how proud he is of my accomplishments.

I would like to thank my <u>Children</u> and <u>all</u> of my <u>Family</u> who have stayed by my side through everything I have experienced in my lifetime. They have remained loyal and shown their devotion to me, whatever path I have traveled. I carried my children as babies, and they now carry me many times, as I grow older.

I have been blessed with <u>Friends</u> that are ever willing to hold me up, when I seem to be falling.

To <u>Everyone</u> who has touched my life with concern and kindness, whether it is family, friends or strangers, I am very grateful.

Foreword

Many writers speak of the role of a therapist as "Teacher" in the process of therapy. I have been a practicing therapist for twenty-three years.

I believe my client, Joanne, is my best teacher. The greatest gifts I have received are through stories shared between us. She has taught me many things during our time together. She has reminded me it is our feelings and attitudes about events that torture us the most.

Joanne has been an example of how each challenge we face prepares us with the opportunity to turn inward and examine our own resources. The trials we endure can bring us face to face with strengths we never imagined. If we accept things as they are, peace is possible.

My heartfelt thanks and gratitude to Joanne for allowing me to share her journey and watch her grow into peacefulness.

—Katie Alfs, M.A., L. P. C.

Acknowledgements

This book <u>is</u> an acknowledgement of my life.

This book <u>states</u> my experiences lived, and my lessons learned.

This book <u>affirms</u> the impact everyone has had on me, and the gratefulness I feel, for what has been given to me.

This book <u>declares</u> the truth of my journey, as I walked in my sandals.

This book <u>encompasses</u> love, for being given the chance to be a part of our world.

This book <u>acknowledges</u> the effect my life has had on me, and on those closest to me.

This book <u>cherishes</u> the gratitude I feel for all those who have made my journey a fulfilling one.

This book <u>embraces</u> the sacredness of family, friendship and the rest of our universe.

This book <u>includes</u> all of the many people who have crossed my path, and what they each individually taught me about my walk here on earth.

This book <u>filled</u> with a Thank You <u>from me to all of you.</u>

1

Katie, My Therapist

To Katie Alfs—who has dragged me kicking and screaming at times to teach me what I needed to learn.

Open my eyes that I may see wondrous things.
—Psalm 119:18

Katie is my therapist whom I *decided* I needed twenty-three years after my mastectomy. She was *not* the first therapist I have seen since my mastectomy, but at this time I was to deal with what more I *needed to learn* and what I *needed to explore* to make *me* feel good again. There were these *unresolved* issues in my life that kept cropping up and trying to surface and I kept *stuffing* them down. The only problem was that they would *not stay* down anymore. And so the *lid* came off of my *box* (as I call it) five years ago.

I worked hard with Katie over these last two years to attempt to *discover* what was going on inside of me. Katie *directed* and *guided* me to a *greater* place of peace. It was not always *easy* to face what was in front of me, and what *I* needed to do to make life better. When the volcano inside of my head erupted that day, it would take me to a *pit of hell* for five years. It has been one of the *darkest* times in my life. I had to *re-visit* places I *did not* want to visit again. I had to *drag* myself through the feelings of my childhood and the lessons I was taught during this time. I had to re-live the *traumas* of my young years to arrive at a place that would bring me *relief.*

So it has been with Katie, at times my *kicking and scream-*

ing, my *sadness* and *disappointment* for what I *thought* life should be, and was not. I have certainly counted my *many blessings* over these last twenty-six years. My choice is to always remain *positive* and be *open* to new learning. I will *continue* to search out the knowledge I need, *to heal,* as life *will* continue to *teach* me, whether I like it or not!

It only matters the *choice* I make to *recognize or dismiss* the many rewards ahead of me, which continues to be—my decision. I *choose* to remain open and let the *light* of new information *shine* in to *show* me the way. Your *choice* is the only requirement also, to a greater sense of *peace and serenity.* In this place of darkness, Katie walked me *slowly* to the *light* at the end of the tunnel.

I am *grateful* for Katie, her knowledge and her desire to help others find a *more* peaceful path. Thank you.

2

My Life after My Mastectomy

For God is at work in you, giving you the will and the power to achieve His purposes.
—Philippians 2:13

My life after my mastectomy has been full of many *blessings* and *grace,* but also a struggle to stay *afloat* at times. I was *challenged* the first several years after surgery to continue to fight those *little* growths that keep wanting to pop up and cause me *unrest.* All of you, who have lived this, know well the story of *waiting* for results from tests and the procedures we endure to see if we are home free again!

I must comment here on this waiting! This wait is such a tremendously difficult time for all involved. Cancer patients and their families *count* the days until the *verdict* is known. This seems *barbaric* to me in this day and age. I think *everyone* of us should *sample* this time of waiting for our loved ones' reports, and maybe we would be a little more understanding of the necessity of reports returning to us on a timely basis. *What a test of Patience!* Except to me, it appears to be just *plain cruelty*!

The doctor stated to me that hopefully things would slow down in the breast that has remained *attached* to me, and I would get some relief from all the worry. Well, I was able to relax after a long period of time and the feeling that I would be alive for a few more years. This *peace* is *priceless,* as one cancer patient to another knows.

I had not been feeling very well for the last five years. It involved *all* of my life, which included my self-esteem, my relationships, and my marriage. I was feeling very depressed and sad, trying to figure out what *I* needed to do to change this very *dark* side of me.

I had continued to think *positive* and try to ward off those *little* cancer cells, that wanted to invade my life. But, somewhere along the way, I became *distracted* in my fight. My life began to take a *different* turn. I was *extremely* bothered by issues of mine that I never felt were *resolved* in my life. I had a great need to take care of *unfinished* business these last five years.

I do know that twenty-six years ago because of raising my family and a busy life, I did not have the *time* to do this or to *mourn my loss.* I would *not* change this beautiful time of raising my children, and all of the *joy* that came from watching them grow into five beautiful adults. My *love* for my children, and my *responsibilities* to them, was my first priority. I believe I accomplished this task pretty well, along with their father's help, when I look at the *type of people* they are today. I Love You.

I have learned that *we do*—what *we do* at that time, because that *is what we know.* We have to realize that when we *beat* ourselves up, we gain *nothing.* One of the greatest reliefs for me is to be able to let myself *off* the hook. I will tell myself that I did *my best,* if this is, in fact the *truth.* This didn't come easy for me, as I am my *greatest* critic. Too many *unrealistic* expectations of myself, I do believe, is one of the biggest reasons that I got myself into this trouble the last five years.

I began to drink more alcohol through these last five years to take away *pain,* discovering as it progressed, that this was *no* way of coping. Life for me became worse, not better. I realized that I was trying to fill a *void* with the abuse of alcohol and yet this *emptiness* in my life became *larger* than me. I realized I needed some *help* to sort out what was going on in my life, and what *I* needed to do about it.

4

We are *brought* to our knees at times, because that is the *only* way—we can *get up*! I was brought to my knees two years ago, when I entered therapy again.

I do believe that most everyone in my life thought that life was good for me, and through *all appearances* it seemed that way. *But not to me.* Sadness *lurked* every day along with *loneliness* and this *void* that remained with me. It was time to figure out what *all* of this was about. When and why had these feelings begun to surface? We know feelings *creep* up on us. They can be so *subtle* and so *slowly* invade our lives that we don't even *realize* it is happening.

This has been my struggle these last five years to replace the *negative* with the *positive* again and rid myself of this *torturous* way of living! I would have to do some *tough* work to figure out what I had *lost* along the way, and *regain* the peace once again, that I so *longed* for.

So has been *MY LIFE AFTER MY MASTECTOMY.*

3

Don't Tell Me How and What to Feel—Just for a While

Only speak when your words are better than your silence.
                                        —Arabic Proverb

I have so struggled with this, *especially* right after my surgery. I would become so *angry* when people would tell me *how* and *what* to feel. They would tell me to be so *grateful* for that *little* tumor that would in fact *take my life,* if it had not been found. I tried to *explain* to them that I did not *feel* so grateful following my surgery. I was too *confused* and *emotionally* tired. I didn't know how to feel the way everyone *thought* I should. So came the *anger* because they wouldn't understand and *listen* to me!

I was worried about my family. My five children were still young and they *needed* me. I was worried that I would be a *burden,* if I did not *get well* and *stay well.* I was *afraid* of what was ahead of me. I was not certain that I could continue to display the *courage* that *everyone* was *expecting* of me. I was *scared* that I would *not* be able to meet the *challenges* of cancer that may lie ahead. I *wanted* to be strong. I *wanted* to be courageous. I *wanted* to remain *positive* in *all* of my thoughts. I *wanted* to show my children that I would be okay, so as they would not worry and have to possibly face the death of their mother.

I couldn't help the feelings of *weakness* and *fatigue* that came over me so *many* times. I was working *diligently* to perform what was *expected* of me.

I didn't know if *cancer* would take my life. I didn't know

6

that a *New Life* was beginning for me. This would be *my challenge,* if I would accept it. I wanted to find a *peaceful path* and *walk the walk* of serenity. After the loss of my breast to cancer, the path was *covered* with thorns and at times I had trouble *finding* the sidewalk! I'll do my best and try so hard to be what I should be—But just for a while—*Don't tell me how and what to feel.*

4

Feel the Pain and Mourn the Loss

When he has tried me, I shall come forth as gold.
                                          —Job 23:10

In this chapter, we will discuss the mourning period that may surely follow after our diagnosis of cancer. We first will deal with the shock of hearing this news, especially when unexpected! We can *read* about how others have coped, contemplate on how to handle this crisis, or we can *talk* about it. We can open some *lines* of communication to *rid* ourselves of fear, worry, loneliness, sadness and the *betrayal* we may feel from our *own* bodies. We need to *communicate* this with our spouse, a good friend or a therapist. This will enhance our *quality* of life and help us to understand our fears and also lessen our loneliness. We must feel a *trust* with whomever we choose to do this with, as our *table* is a *delicate* and *vulnerable* one. It is important to our physical and mental well being that our feelings and questions do *not* remain bottled up inside of us. *We must mourn our loss.* We *cannot* be willing to stay stuck in that revolving door that takes us *nowhere but in circles.* We must *break* loose to move forward again. It is okay to say that we are hurting, whether that be physical, emotional or *both.* A valuable lesson that I have learned was spoken by Oprah—she states: "My pain is *no greater than yours,* and *yours is no greater than mine."*

We will *not measure* the pain, we will just tell others, *we are in pain.* We are certainly *not* feeling comfortable with ourselves and/or our bodies. If we check the *hyphenation* in the dictionary of this word disease, it shows it to be written

8

as—*dis-ease.* This seems to be an *appropriate* description for those fears and sadness that come with this diagnosis. It also relays to others, those thoughts that we now *carry* with us. I must *now* give myself *permission* to—

FEEL THE PAIN AND MOURN OUR LOSS.

5

Be Vigilant and Aware of Growth

Let us not look back in anger or forward in fear, but around in awareness.

—James Thurber

Together, God and I are creating my ongoing, wondrous life story.

—*Daily Word*—Unity Village

We do need to be *vigilant* in working with, and through our cancer diagnosis, even though we may *not* know for sure the outcome. It is impossible to know what is in *store* for us, but we *can* believe that we are doing *our best*. Life is not a *contest* to see how people react to this diagnosis. We all have our *own* way of dealing with our challenges in life. We just need to *stay aware* of our feelings, and *monitor* our worries and fears. We attempt to keep these worries and fears in a *safe* place of trust with whomever we *choose* to allow into this part of our life.

We need to look around and see the potential for *growth* and *healing* in our minds and bodies. We may need to make *peace* with someone. We may need to say we are *sorry*. We may need to make *restitution* regarding some other circumstance that we have failed to make right. In doing these things, we will feel better, *just in case,* something happens to us, and we don't have a second chance.

This doesn't have to be the day after our diagnosis, but just allow these thoughts to sink into our subconscious. We don't have to hurry, but we need to find a way to complete these tasks, so our *healing* can take place in our *soul*. As we move to a different *level* in our being, we will *complete* what has to be done. We *will* come to a greater understanding of the effect our cancer has had on us. A purpose? Yes—The *road* that took us to our *soul*.

We are only asked to *remain* vigilant and aware of our growth. Give ourselves credit for the *good* job we are doing and working hard to accomplish our goals that we have set out to hopefully see to completion.

With this *acceptance, calm* and *peace—We Find Our Soul.*

6

"Listen to Me"—I Have Something to Say

Robbing life of friendship is like robbing the world of sun.
—Cicero

Today, I want to *state* my feelings and fears. Not in a *negative* manner but to tell you about what I have lived and experienced. *It's only the facts.* The facts can't be negative, *if told in a positive light*, and with *hope* for the future.

I couldn't at the time of my mastectomy predict my future, and I still cannot. Today, I *am* able and willing to share my life after my mastectomy and the experiences that I have encountered to explain where this disease has brought me.

I felt many times that others would *not* listen. I thought they would not try to understand what *I had to say*. But I have realized, so many things at the time of my cancer diagnosis, *I did not know*. How could I? I hadn't *lived* it yet.

We become experienced *after* we *live* the experience. Isn't that the way with most everything in life? Don't we have to *walk* in each other's shoes to *really* know? The *best* we can do to *help* each other is to show empathy and just *try* to understand. The only *requirement* at times is to *listen*.

Don't *judge me* or tell me what *you* would do. You *don't* know. I *didn't know* either until I *walked* this path that was dealt to me.

Remember the old Indian Proverb—"Walk a mile in my moccasins, and then judge me."

It's okay if at times *you* don't know what to *say* to me. *I understand.* I only want you to *sit* with me, *hold my hand,* put your arm *around* me, let me *lay* my head on your shoulder

12

and cry. *Cry* with me if you want. I will *welcome* your tears. Lend me your strength *freely* when I ask this of you. I'll just *borrow* your strength for a while, until *I* am stronger again. *Share* with me your feelings. I can take it. Tell me the *truth* about your fears and concerns too. I *want* to hear them. This brings us *closer* together. This makes our *sorrow and pain* clearer, and *creates* more understanding between us. These are the *gifts* we give to each other. This is the way we *display* our love for each other and takes us *both* to our soul.

Please listen to me—*I HAVE SOMETHING TO SAY.*

7

Men—Just a Few Minutes of Your "Time"—How Important Can That Be?

As I turn to God for the solution, I am gently guided to what is right for me.

*—Daily Word—*Unity Village

This book is all about women and the diagnosis of cancer. I believe it needs to include a chapter for the *men* in our lives and their role, in order for them to stay *connected* to us, *with love. Women*—we need to *communicate* our feelings, for men to understand how our *sharing* with each other will bring *us* to a place of peace. This *battle* with cancer is a *family* affair. Cancer patients cannot *shut* others out, and *expect* them to try to figure out our *needs.* None of us are mind readers, and we shouldn't have to be, as this becomes so *painful* for all of *us.*

Men—I place this chapter at this point in time, because *time* is what we are going to talk about. It is what is *needed* by a cancer patient and follows right *after* our cancer diagnosis. This writing is about a *season.* A period of time in our recovery for the men closest to us to display their *devotion.*

I want to say to the *men* in our lives that we women know you are different than us. You are *wired* to *find* solutions to *all* of our problems. You can *free* yourself of finding the *answer* to this *pain.* Don't *waste* your time on this one. *GOD* is the boss and in *charge* of this outcome. HE is the *decision* maker. HE only asks us to *trust* HIM and to continue to pray for *ourselves* and our *loved* ones.

Cancer is a *lonely* disease. This diagnosis *blasts* us out of the *ballpark.* I'm sitting in the *bleachers* of life, surrounded by many—*but alone!* My *safety* is threatened. My *comfort* is rocked. I want to *participate* in life's *holy* game, but I'm *scared* now! I feel *uncertain* about my future? I'm *afraid* of what lies ahead of me!

After a cancer diagnosis, *we* struggle to find the answer to all of this confusion. We are *trying* to *accept* God's *will* for us. We certainly are feeling fragile, sensitive, and vulnerable. Cancer proves to be one of the *deadliest* discussions we will ever have with our doctor.

Men—this is when you *step up* to the *plate* and *show us* what you can do. What women are asking for at this time—is *not* very complicated. Our *needs* consist of Love, Understanding, Compassion, Caring and a little *Time.* Yes, just a *little* time may seem a strange request, but it is *crucial* to our healing. The *"Good News"* is—it only has to be a *few minutes.* It can be a *gentle* touch, a *kiss* on the cheek, a *loving* pat on the back. Any gesture, that lets me know that *you* are there for *me.*

Men—the cancer patient speaks, "But, oh, I'll *never* really be able to put into words and describe what those *loving touches* from him meant to *me!*" They were so *comforting* and made *me* feel *warm* all over. I think your *loving hands* even *take* away a bit of *pain.*

Touching is so powerful, but many of us are *not* comfortable with it. Maybe, we have not *witnessed* this display of power in *our* life, or have not been shown, by example. For that matter, we don't know the *feeling* of security it gives us, also. Let's just *try* it and see what happens? Just *force* yourself to *touch* and see the *response* from me. It will get *easier* the more you *practice.* I think *you* may be surprised that it also makes *you* feel good. You have *nothing* to lose, and so *much* to gain.

Men shout—"They are *sorry,* but sometimes *time* is so

valuable." "I can't *give* more!" "That's *all* the time I have!" In frustration, I have heard men's voices repeating and repeating, "I have to do so much *juggling* every day to meet *so* many needs."

We *all* do our *best*, after a cancer diagnosis, to try to carry on through this time of *challenge* and *sorrow* in the family. Everyone should *pitch* in and act from their *heart*. This is a *trying* game for all of us. *Men* feel they *must* meet their job responsibilities. This is their commitment and duty, and yet lies the tremendous burden to *protect* the whole family and take care of *everyone*.

"Men"—this *is* a *blessed* opportunity of a lifetime, and it may only come *once*. Don't *wait*—just a *few* minutes—you will *not* have to *suffer* sadness and guilt later, in realizing you *did* give *me* what I asked of *you*.

"Time is of the essence." I think that means, *"Hurry Up!"* Also, *these* statements—"I succeeded because the *opportunity* presented itself and "the *timing was just right!"* "Time is running out," falls into the *emergency* category and I'm sure we have heard this phrase spoken often.

> *For everything there is a season—a time for every purpose*
> *under Heaven. A time to weep, and a time to laugh.*
> —Ecclesiastes 3:1, 4

I was thinking about the baseball *season* seeming so short. I like to watch it, but it goes so *fast*—just like the *holy game* of life that flies by. I hear the PITCHER in this game is really good. HE certainly has been the one in *control* of that ball through this *holy* season—(sorry I mean)—*whole* season.

In that last game I played, I *decided* to swing at that pitch and *knew* it was the *wrong* thing to do. I gave up my chances for *winning*. Do we sometimes know, at times we are *not* putting forth the effort and showing our love in this *holy* game? That fly ball was *caught!* The game is *over!*

I won't be too *harsh* on myself. I'll do *better* tomorrow. I will have *another* opportunity, to *try* harder. Although, I do want to give my *best* with what I *know* about this game—(of life). What I have heard about this PITCHER kind of *scares* me. HE is *really* good!

Oh, boy! I'm up to bat *again*. This *game* is really an *important* one.

Everyone is counting on me! *The bases are loaded!*

This *season* of life just took on a *strange twist*.

My *loved one* just became a *statistic*—a diagnosis of cancer!

I wonder how I will *deal* with this diagnosis? This *hit* really threw me *off* base! My plans for this *holy* game of life weren't supposed to confront me with all of these *important* decisions! I'll have to find a *new* strategy for my *game*, and do some things *differently*. It seems I will have to *change* the way I have been *playing* ball. This *is* hardball in the *holy* game of life! I am going to have to *practice* even harder with what I *know*, and have *learned* up until this point in *time*—to make me a *winner!*

I'd better get *practicing* here and see what *I* can do to be a *champion*, in my *loved* one's eyes. I don't want to be *out* in *left field*, and *not be aware* of what I could have done to help *win* in this *holy game* of life. I want to be recognized as a *team* player. This baseball season is not a *lengthy* one, but neither is life. I want to read up on those *Stats*—and *listen* to see how others *improved* their *batting* average and were *recognized* when they *found* success, and reached the *top* of their game.

The *scoreboard* is reflecting the *innings* left to play. Time *is* running out! My *team* is up to bat! My *family* is watching my *performance* in this *big park* filled with so many people! They *are* aware of my reactions in this *arena* of cancer. They are *counting* on me to *teach* them. I want to *practice*—what I *preach!* I could take the *first* pitch—or—wait? I know what I'll do!

I'll just *swing* from my *heart.* I *can't* go wrong! Wow! The *umpire* sure won't have trouble making this *call!* I just hit a *grand slam* right out *into* those *bleachers!* I can even take a *few extra minutes* to run the bases. No way is my *family*—(another mistake)—I meant *team* going to *lose* this game, after all the *effort* and *work* we have put forth. My *practicing* of loving *touches* did pay off. That ball *touched* my bat just where it counts. My *family* and I are *champions.*

I'm *still* in the *bleachers* watching you—but—I'm not *alone* now—*I* was just *blessed* by *you.* It seems like you *hit* that ball, and *aimed* it right towards *me.* I know the hard work you have done—*just for me*—to make sure you *didn't* strike out! Your timing was *great! I* just *caught* your home run ball—and it *only* took—just a *few minutes* of your time.

Without a doubt, we are influenced by others around us, and those that so *closely* surround us, after our diagnosis of cancer. This is a good reason to try to make our actions and our behavior in the *short* periods of time we have, so *worthwhile.* In their recovery, cancer patients don't *ever* forget what was done for them, and who was *willing* to give of *their* time.

My prayers and my love enhance my relationships with others.

—*Daily Word*—Unity Village

Following in the footsteps of Jesus, I am compassionate and caring.

Daily Word—Unity Village

Through my acts of caring, I am an expression of God's love made visible.

Daily Word—Unity Village

8

Children—Let Them Come into Our Hearts or Hold Tight on the Reins as Protecting Parents

Let the little children come to me; do not stop them; for it is to such as these, that the Kingdom of God belongs.
—Mark 10:14

A God who became so small, and came, as a baby could only be full of Love and Mercy.
—St. Therese

Serving the need of others brightens each day.
—Douglas M. Lawson

Loving and *good* parents are always trying to *protect* their children. We have all heard from their little mouths, in their growing-up years these statements: I'm old enough!—Everyone else can do it!—Their parents don't care—You always try to shelter me!—Why, won't you let me grow up?—You treat me like a baby! You are so protective!

My children had this *famous* line—*"Don't worry—I know what I am doing."*

When the fourth and fifth child came along, and I heard the *same* story line, I knew then, it had to be a *genetic* thing that they *all* had *acquired* from birth. This seems to *begin* at quite an *early* age and *continues* on until they have found their *own* place to *live.* Our *caring* and *protection* of our children is *born* out of *love.* We have to *realize* that the children *don't* know this yet, and won't until they are about twenty-one years of age.

Our discussion in this chapter talks about the children and their involvement in our cancer diagnosis. Sometimes, we will learn that *protecting*—(by *not* sharing) is not *rewarding* for anyone. This is what makes this time of cancer and recovery so *difficult*, especially for those moms out there. It becomes an attempt to direct our thinking to a 360-degree angle. We are *not* accustomed to taking care of our children in this fashion. We *want* to protect them from *all* hurt and harm.

All of a sudden, a cancer diagnosis comes! We are supposed to figure out what is *good* for the children to *know, how much,* and what *not* to tell them?

Of course, the ages of the children certainly make a difference concerning our *level* of sharing with them. We must be *careful* that we do not make them *more* afraid, than they already are. What a job!

My children at the time of my mastectomy were; 19, 18, 16, 14, 7½. The youngest being too young to *understand* much of what everyone was getting so *terribly* sad and upset about. She did not realize, as the older children did, what a devastating diagnosis cancer is. I use the word *devastating not* with negative connotation, but for us to realize the *depth* of sadness, and to *demonstrate* the understanding needed from us, as to the effect our diagnosis of cancer has had on our children *also.* This may very well be *their* greatest challenge in life. We *need* to *include* the children in our recovery and recognize what a *critical* role they play in our *healing.* They look for *recognition* and their *importance,* as this is a *family* affair. Their *memory* of this time will no doubt last a lifetime. But, before you begin to beat yourselves up over what you *didn't* do, remember the good times and what you *did* do out of love for your family. How are we supposed to know all of what we *should have* or *could have* done? Here comes those *two words*—should have—could have—that will make us *all* crazy if we *allow* them into our vocabulary and our life!

It is never *too late,* even if this time of recovery is *thankfully* ended for you. We can communicate *now* with our children. Tell them how *you* felt. Tell the children that you were scared too, and *worried* about them. Tell them you *love* them, and, Oh! *like me,* tell them you would do some things *differently,* just because you are now *graced* with *more* wisdom.

Cancer patients do *understand* the struggle, as we don't know the *big picture* of where all of this is going to take us. We *don't* have the control, nor are we going to. This is all *new* to everyone who is involved. We are *all* scared! The children sense this nervousness and the *chaos* that is occurring in our household. They are *afraid* of being left, and this makes their *hearts* heavy. This is why it is so necessary to do what we can to *assure* them of their safety and security. The only trouble being that sometimes we are so *tired* and *weary,* we can't *think* straight! We are wrapped up in ourselves, *not* a selfish wrapping, but *clothed* in such sadness, anxiety, worry, and our search for *HOPE.* We *need* a reason to push forward and carry on with *everyday* life. The *children become so much a part of this reason.*

I have so often thought, particularly right after my diagnosis of cancer, when I would pray. I'd start *talking* to God. Then my question would be, "Why did you give me five children, and now *YOU* are *not* going to give me *enough* time to raise them?" I was sad and depressed because I wanted *more* time to make sure *they* were *okay* with life! I *so* struggled with this issue. I then had to *begin* to accept and change that *thinking* of mine. This was not *easy* for me, as I had expected to *take care* of them, at least to their adult years. "The children *need* me," I told God. "Can't *YOU* see that?"

My prayers were *not* on the highest level of *reverence* many times. I believe we call this the (anger) part of our cancer diagnosis!

I realized after *many* prayers, meditation, and therapy that I had to *Let go and Let God.* So then comes the *compromise*—okay, I think my *older* children will be able to *survive* without me, but how about the *younger ones?* Who will take *care* of them the way *I* do? I couldn't say these things to my children. If I'm that *scared,* think of what it would *do* to *them*?

Then comes the *acceptance* of it all! I *can't* do anything about it. I can only *trust* that I have done a good job up *until* now, if this is *all* the time I have. I didn't know the *Big Plan* for my life, but then none of us do. These *deep* thoughts and sadness are part of what makes cancer such a *lonely* disease. We can't just *blurt* these feelings out, and everyone wonders—how is *she* going to *make it* through this crisis? A cancer patient *gropes* for answers and *cries* for their children. I know! I was *one* of them twenty-six years ago.

It will not be *surprising* to you then, that your children want to be a part of your *recovery.* They want to *share* in this time, and show their *love.* They can't do this if we *don't* let them into our hearts, and *include* them. They are fearful and anxious also, *hearing* this diagnosis of cancer. They are much *wiser* and more *loving* than we may want to *believe.* I have *witnessed* this in my own life with *my* children at the time of my mastectomy. They seem to want to stay *close* to you, and feel your *presence. Help them*—by a kiss, a hug, talking, or some reassurance that you are struggling to *get well* and *stay well.* When the children ask you questions about your cancer, answer them *honestly.* Including them in our recovery will help to alleviate *more* fears. Your cancer has also *shaken* their world!

Would I do some things differently? *Sure,* I would. I am wiser today, but as we all know—*hindsight* is 20/20. It is quite a bit *easier* for me to *give* really *good* advice, after I've already *lived* the experience—*in comes* the wisdom! *Wisdom* is gained *after* living the experience, as everything *is* in life. Doesn't that seem *backwards?* We don't want to feel sorry and sad *after* the challenges are *over*! Well, we *can't* do anything about that, can we? All *we* can do is our *best* and letting everyone know, that *is* what we are doing!

I was thinking about the *gifts* I received from my children, *after* my surgery. My daughter would bring over my favorite cookies from the bakery. A phone call from another one of the children, asking, how I was feeling today? I would be asked by all of them at individual times, if there was something they could do for me? Would you like a cup of coffee or tea? Are you hungry? Something to eat? One of the children would just sit on my bed, and talk a while.

These are the *blessings* our children give to us, because they *don't* know what to do. *They* just want us to be *free* of pain and *comfortable* again.

My grown children know today that they *cannot* change the outcome of a diagnosis of cancer, but they sure will *fight the fight* right along side of anyone who *asks* this of them.

Should we *hold tight* on the *reins* as parents and know what is *best* for the children? Do we see the need to *extend* those reins of *protection* and *control* and give them the *freedom* to *act* from their *hearts*?

Remember that *genetic* trait that my kids passed along to each other?

You know—that favorite *line* they *all* spoke many years ago.

"Don't worry—I know what I am doing."

I knew what they were up to *then*, but it appears my children are *practicing* this *principle* today. It is what they wanted *me* to *believe* was good for them *and* me, in their growing-up years, but it couldn't be—because I had to *pro-*

tect them. It seems—that *statement of theirs* is filled with devotion, dedication, determination, and decisions. All of these *acts* of *freedom* by them are from their *hearts* today, and display their *own* belief in themselves, as adults.

I think they were really *on to* something as *little* people; they just had to get *taller.*

Don't worry!—(Be Still)—*I know what I am doing.*—(Know that I am God.)

BE STILL AND KNOW THAT I AM GOD.
—Psalm 46:10

This is what I *hear* and *see*—about *how* my children *feel* and *what* they *do* today.

I HEAR TODAY—freely talking about cancer and the ramifications of this disease.
I HEAR TODAY—the sadness in their voices when another is diagnosed.
I HEAR TODAY—only a desire to help others.
I HEAR TODAY—asking the question—what can I do?
I HEAR TODAY—advocating mammograms and screening for *all* cancers.
I HEAR TODAY—about cards received by ill people, and how it made their day.
I HEAR TODAY—their understanding of the feelings of a cancer diagnosis.
I HEAR TODAY—when a cancer patient tells me that my children, their spouses, and my grandchildren stepped up to help a cancer patient, and said nothing about it to anyone.

25

I SEE TODAY—the look on their faces when word of another cancer diagnosis.

I SEE TODAY—the sadness on their faces, when another will undergo treatments.

I SEE TODAY—the kindness shown to others.

I SEE TODAY—the meal being brought in to make it easier on the family.

I SEE TODAY—the prayers so freely said for cancer patients and their families.

I SEE TODAY—their willingness to go the extra mile for anyone, if need be.

I SEE TODAY—their learning and teaching others what to do, by their example.

What I *Don't Hear Today*—from my children, is any complaints for their *time given*, to fight the fight of a diagnosis of cancer.

What I *Don't See Today*—from my children, is the earlier sadness on their faces, *only joy and gratitude*, when another one of us wins the battle.

9

If That Beautiful Old Kitchen Table Could Talk

Friendship is the only cement that will hold the world together.
—Jo Petty

It isn't what you know, but what you are willing to learn.
—Cliff Schimmels

The smallest good deed is better than the grandest intention.
—Unknown

Our beautiful old *family* kitchen table was bought forty-one years ago. I looked at it one day and got to thinking about what a *story* this table has to *tell*. This place of eating, drinking, and being merry *holds* much more than the *joys* of family and friends. I think if it *could* talk, it would go something like this:

Wow! There sure have been a lot of people that have sat around me. I'm glad the mother and father decided to get two more chairs and make it six. It was getting pretty *crowded* over the years. They seem to add more and more people into this family. I sure think they were wise in getting a *Formica* top for me, with all of this *use* I get. I sure have *noticed* that when the children come; they all seem to have their *own* seat. One night they were all here as a family, and it was getting pretty busy. It appears to me that when there are extra people, the children seem to squeeze in another chair, but it is as close to *their* spot as they can get.

27

When the children were very young, I heard their parents talking to them one day, and telling them that their seat at the table is *very* important, and *represents* their *place* in the family. They *always* took the seat that had been assigned to them, as they moved from the highchair to the youth chair and then to the *big* table. The children were told that this shows *respect* and *honor* for each other, as *special* people. This seating arrangement continued all through their growing up years. It seems like they all took it to *heart*, because God *help* the sibling who is in another's chair! Sometimes, I have seen where they just *look* at each other, and movement takes place! What a *respect* these children have for each other. When the mother and father told them their *chair* was just for *them* around the family table, there was no *doubt* in my mind, they were *believers!*

I heard their parents teaching them that they should *never* be *impolite* and *demand* their space, when *company* is here! The children do *shuffle* a lot of chairs around though, when there is a *crowd* here. It seems if they don't get the *exact* spot they claim as theirs, they sure get as *close* as they can. I've even seen where they *squeeze* a chair in between two chairs in *their* area. There is *not* much commotion or any *nastiness* that is occurring through this procedure. It seems all of this is done with an *ease* of spirit. They all just—move over—out—in—sideways—back up—go forward—whatever it takes and no one says much of anything about it. It seems that all understand what the others' plan is, and they *fully* understand what is going on. I don't think they even *realize* themselves what they do and how they do it? It is quite interesting, to say the least! The conversation with everyone *continues* in a polite manner, even through all of this juggling. I have also seen where one of the children sits down for just a *second* to chat; the other one comes along and just *motions* to them—*to move over. Silence* again, no argument, the sibling *moves,* and the conversation continues as normal, without *missing* a beat!

This is quite an *amazing* feat, now that the family has *grown* so much over the years, since I *first* arrived. They were so *little* then, and sure didn't take up *much* room. You would think with all of this wear and tear, I would be so *ready* to be *refinished!* Well, it's like this. I have only been *redone* once in all of these years! I know you are *amazed,* and actually so am I. I think I have *discovered* why.

Every one of the children, family members, and *this* families' friends have all been at my *table,* one time or another. Some have been there *alone,* others with *some* of the family, and *some* many more times than the rest. The mother seems to know what is going to happen when a person *sits* down, because she immediately goes to *get* the *box* of Kleenex off of the desk in the kitchen. Now, I did hear a couple of times when one of the children were there *alone,* they looked around, and asked the mom—where *was* the box of Kleenex? I guess the mom just didn't move *fast* enough that day. Now, at these times, I can be *pretty* sure there will be some *crying* going on. Sometimes it is *more* than other times. It just *depends* on their struggles and challenges. It is really something to see how *everyone* who is involved with the person crying, is *always* so supportive. My table is *overflowing* with tears, love and caring. So I have decided that there is a *solution* in our *crying* eyes that *protects* this finish on my table.

Maybe, it is in *finding* a *solution* to their problems and heartaches that keeps me *looking good.* Although, they still do polish me, in spite of all of these tears, I remain in *good condition.* I believe, because of the *tears,* which are connected to secrets told, a new story, listening, communicating, and knowing their *importance* will never be violated or disrespected, I remain *intact* and so do *they.* When asking for advice from all of these *loving* people that sit here, it seems the *love* given so freely, works as a *preservative* for *me* and for *them.*

I guess if something was sold in a *can* with *tear solution* in it, these business people selling polish might go *out* of business. These tears don't *cost* anything in dollars, but they sure are *valuable* when they are *shared.*

I've mentioned *my discovery* concerning my theory about me staying in such *good shape.* I think *all of the above* is why I was *stripped down* only once. What I noticed also is, when I see these *same* people afterwards sitting at *my* table again, they seem to be pretty *preserved* themselves, and *happier* now. Maybe, I should pass *myself* around and *visit* with other families. I don't want to *brag or boast,* but maybe—I could *suggest* to others—to buy a table *just like me*!

10

Rehab for Me?—You've Got to Be Kidding!

Life with Christ is an endless hope; without Him, a hopeless end.
                                                      —Merv Rosell

Faith is being able to see with your heart, what you cannot see with your eyes.
                                                      —Robert C. Savage

What do we know about the word *Intervention*? We have heard it used in reference to people who *needed* help. These *types* of people seem to need a *nudge* or sometimes even a *push* from another. What is your opinion on this *method* of helping someone else? Certainly, I am not asking anyone to sit in the seat of *judgment* that we sometimes *decide* to climb up on, and pretend to be *all knowing*. I am referring to a kindness and a caring shown by *us* to a *loved* one, in hopes we can help *them* find a better way of life. This is what my children *wished* for me.

I never imagined in my wildest dreams that I would be *involved* in an *intervention* from *my* children for *abuse* of alcohol. I was *one* of the children sitting with *my* mom many years ago *begging* her to go into a hospital to receive some help and good care, which she *deserved*. I had been *involved* in this conversation with her many times. She was repeatedly hospitalized in my growing-up years, and I knew the *sadness* of an intervention. Now, I was sitting on the other side of the fence!

It was a Sunday morning, October of 2001, when the

phone rang and it was my youngest daughter asking if she and her sisters could come over to talk to me. The children certainly knew that I had not been *feeling* very well, or *functioning* very well. The children's greatest concern was all that was going on in my life, and the way I was *dealing* with it. I had turned to the *abuse* of alcohol to get *through* it. All of us who use or have used this method to *cover* the *pain in our lives know full well it gets us nowhere fast! Alcohol never solved* anything yet—and *never* will.

Being raised in and suffering the devastation of living in an alcoholic home, *coping* this way was not for *me*! I had *decided* as a very young person that my children's way of life would *not* include any of this *pain*. Alcohol was *not* a part of my life for *many* years. I was too busy raising my family and taking care of my home. I was *happy* doing this and expending my *efforts* on my family. So what happened in the later years?

Along came the tumultuous last six years! Now, don't get *me* wrong. The AA program is an *honest* one. I have had to *admit* that I had drank too much many times and I *knew* that. But, what I also *know* is that the drinking was *different* for me the last six years. Those of us who have experienced this know what I am talking about. *No excuses* for any *over* drinking by anyone, only be aware that drinking can take a *turn* at some point and *become* a greater problem. It was used *differently* and more often to *cover* the *deep* pain for me. There is help *Out There* for anyone of us. I believe that one of the most *sacred* moments at an AA meeting is the beginning, when we take a few minutes to *pray* for those still *suffering* from this disease. We explain it as being *Out There,* when active drinking is occurring. Think about it—*Out there is—No Where*!

All alone. Just sadness and sorrow. Feeling shame and

disgrace. Reach out and pick up *that* telephone. There are so many caring people *ready* to help *you—Out There.*

My *Intervention* on that Sunday morning was filled with much emotion. My daughters arrived, all coming at the *same* time. They seemed *nervous.* I *knew* their fear, as I have been there myself *many* times before.

As they gathered together, they headed right for that beautiful *old* kitchen table, that I talked to you about in the previous chapter. For some reason that morning, I did *not* want to sit there. I didn't really know *why.* I just felt that we *needed* to sit in our living room where there is *more space* for everyone. For the first time, the kitchen table seemed like it would be too *crowded*! Isn't that insane thinking, especially because that old table of mine is so *full* of love and concern?

This day seemed to be different. I believe it was because my children were talking to *me* about *me*! I was *not* in *charge* of anything on that day, except, my *own* life. Maybe that old table always places *me* in a spot of comfort, and now I was on *the spot,* and in the *spotlight*!

Our living room is a *peaceful* room and *holds* many *special* memories. The sun reflects into the living room from the large dining room windows and *spreads* sunshine onto that dining room table that has *held* so many of us. Maybe, there was *more freedom* for my children that morning in the living room, as they *struggled* to begin their conversation and their *intervention* with me.

INTERVENTION: the act or fact of interfering with a condition to modify it, or with a process to *change* its course.

This definition seems *pretty simple,* doesn't it? Just *change* what you are doing, and everything will come out *all right*! Take on a *different* course for your life, and your life will be *on course*! This is what others *want* us to do. This is certainly what we *need* to do if our life is *spinning* out of control! I am *not* happy abusing alcohol. *I'm sad.* I don't want *my* children to *worry* about me all the time. I *lived* that life of worry for many years, and it is a *tortuous* way of life. It makes the children feel *helpless* and *hopeless.* All of these events that have taken place to make my children be so *concerned* about me were *not* part of my plan for *my* life, nor for *their* life. I sure didn't map out this *direction* for *my* family.

We have two tall chairs that sit in front of our fireplace in our living room. On Christmas Eve, when the whole family gathers, the kids have always put their presents to Ron and me from them in front of these chairs. This is where we sit with the family to open gifts and share with each other. Interestingly, they have *chosen* on this difficult Sunday morning to sit today where they always do on the beautiful eve of Christmas. I have just discovered this, in looking at our living room, while writing this. The children are more comfortable when they are feeling their *importance* and the *confidence* they have gained, within themselves.

As my children began to speak to me, tears came very soon from *all* of us. I believe they *rehearsed* what they were going to say, because this *is* who they are. They were *gentle.* They were *kind.* They displayed no *harsh* judgment of me. They *expressed* their deep *concern* and *love* for my well-being. They relayed to me the *desire* they all had to see me a *happy* person again.

What were *all* of my children *saying* that day? *They wanted their mother back!*

The mother who *decided* many years ago that this *type* of pain would *not* enter our life and/or control it.

They wanted the person who *planned* a good life for all of us, not free of *problems,* but *free* of alcohol.

The children were *asking* for the mother they didn't *worry* so much about, and *wonder* if she is doing okay today?

They hoped this person—who became a *different* person, would become the mother they once had.

The children were not being *selfish* in their *requests*. They just *wanted* us to be the family that we *used* to be—with the mother who *used* to be.

The mother who, *somehow*, even in *my* silence, the children *knew* and *felt*, what I had *prayed* and *promised* for myself and for them. A life and our home to be full of *safety* and *security*. This I had *decided*, so many years ago.

My children did such a beautiful job of *stating* their love and concern.

All of their *efforts* shown to me that day were added *grace* to my soul.

I *love* them for their *individual* blessings each one has given to me, which make them the *unique* child they are, and *impossible* to replace.

And so—I entered Rehab on October 19, 2001.

11

Needed—a Place of Peace and Serenity

As a mother comforts her child, so I will comfort you.
                                                    —Isaiah 66:13

Now to him who by the power at work within us is able to accomplish abundantly far more than all we can ask or imagine, to him be glory.
                                                    —Ephesians 3:20–21

This may sound strange to some, but I am referring to a facility that is called a *REHABILITATION CENTER.*

I have just come home from 8 days in this *House of Wonder.* I agreed to enter this facility, because of my *mismanagement* of alcohol and, the *Intervention* by my children, which I spoke about in the previous chapter.

I knew I was becoming *powerless* and choosing to use this drug to *cope* with life. As my life felt *out* of control—

I needed this drug to hold on to and function (I thought)?

It becomes your friend (I thought)?

Friends are there to *HELP* each other through the *good* and *bad* of life.

If it was helping me, why did I feel so helpless?
If it was helping me, why did I feel so hopeless?
If it was helping me, why did I feel so sad?
If it was helping me, why did I feel so lonely?
If it was helping me, why did I feel so isolated?

If it was helping me, why did I feel so guilty?
If it was helping me, why did I feel so shameful?
If it was helping me, why did I feel so afraid?
If it was helping me, why did I feel so insecure?
If it was helping me, why did I feel so ugly?
If it was helping me, why did I feel so angry?
If it was helping me, why did I feel so enraged?

I wonder the definition of a FRIEND?
My family doesn't make me *feel* this way.
My good friends don't make me *feel* this way.
My nice new friends don't make me *feel* this way.

This disease is a very difficult one for most of us to understand. Just stop it, and you will get well! We don't realize that some of us don't know how. The people I observed in their struggle to fight off this *disease,* are not *bad* people. They are like everyone else we *love* and *treasure.* They didn't ask for this *demon* to be a part of their lives. It is *Satan's* work, and he sure does grab a hold on us. He is very *unwilling* to let go of our bodies, minds, and spirit.

I *watched* loving, caring and *sincere* people struggle, with their attempt to ward off the ramifications of this *ugly* culprit, called *Alcohol.* These *special* people shook, cried, and prayed. Their skin was painted yellow, as their liver rebelled. Some half asleep from medication, to help make them well. They wanted to stay awake and listen, to *learn* more about themselves. I *watched* some vow to *never* drink again, and some that knew if they did, it meant *death.*

I decided to ask myself this question during my stay at this place of comfort—how can anyone call Alcohol a *Friend*?

This has been a *part* of my learning that came from the Rehabilitation Center—A house that will lead you to a place of peace and serenity, *if you only desire it.*

12

I'm Sorry—How Many Times Can I Say It?

Forgiveness does not mean that you continue to put yourself at risk, nor are you obligated to struggle with the other person's issues.

—Dr. Laura Schlessinger

Never let a problem become an excuse!
—Crystal Cathedral Calendar—2002

Anybody who dares to try will never be a total failure.
—Crystal Cathedral Calendar—2002

Then he said to the man, "Stretch out your hand." He stretched it out, and it was restored as sound as the other.
—Matthew 12:13

Only two words, and yet what a *powerful* punch they pack!

Are these *power* words in your vocabulary, or do you choose to *wait* and *see* what the other person's plan is, and the effect it will have on you?

"I'm sorry" were not words I heard in my growing up years. Therefore, this statement of my feelings *did not* come naturally to me. They *seemed* awkward. I am *not* in my comfort zone and actually, feel *uncomfortable* speaking them. Words we did not hear used, in our young years, appear foreign to us. We can then understand that "I'm sorry" is a *teaching* and a *gift*, given to us by our parents or caretakers. Children are *taught* by seeing, hearing, and by example. Could these statements below be the reason why, I am afraid to *use* these two words and feel I may *become* too vulnerable?

I'm sorry could mean—I was *wrong.*
I'm sorry could mean—I may have *misjudged.*
I'm sorry could mean—I may have *jumped* the gun in my interpretation.
I'm sorry could mean—I may have to *analyze* the situation again.
I'm sorry could mean—I did not *communicate* properly.
I'm sorry could mean—I did make you *wonder* about my intent to hurt.
I'm sorry could mean—I did question and *assume* your intent was to hurt.

I have *felt* these two powerful words *swell* up inside of me, but *didn't* or *couldn't* speak them many times, in my younger years.

This created: *sadness* in my heart, *discomfort* in my soul, and my *wonder* about missing my chance to make something right. My *arrogance* that I would have to admit—I may be wrong, questioning my misjudgment of *your* intent, lack of my explaining, *my* intent. Doesn't it appear that *all* of this becomes so *complicated*? This could be the reason why it is so *difficult* for us to get these two words out of our mouths.

If we are *willing* to recognize when they are *needed,* attempt to *blurt* the words out, and *most* importantly, *practice* using this phrase in our daily life, we will find it begins to come with a greater ease and so natural over time. Our *sincerity* and *apology* will come from our hearts. Believe me, we really *won't* care after a while, who *is* the *exact* culprit. After my *practicing* now for *so* long, it is much *easier* for me to say, "I'm sorry." It becomes just a *part* of your everyday life, *without* any discomfort. We then will be *honoring* and displaying our *respect* for one another. We will look to each other *knowing* and *accepting,* our strengths and weaknesses.

I'm sorry for all those times
that I didn't say
I'm sorry.

13

Cancer Is Called the "Big C"—Can Other "Big C" Words Cause Us Harm?

Every valley shall be lifted up, and every mountain and hill be made low; the uneven ground shall become level, and the rough places a plain.

—Isaiah 40:4

Awakened to God's presence, I greet today's possibilities with enthusiasm.

—*Daily Word*—Unity Village

1. *CONTROL* MAY WORK ITS WAY INTO YOUR LIFE VERY SUBTLY.

It leaves you with *no* options. You give your power to *choose* away. You are *taken over* by a monster that will not be *quieted*, until his/her way is met. When we allow this to be done to us, we *lose* ourselves.

2. *COMPROMISE* IS BORN OUT OF LOVE—IT IS A GIVE AND TAKE.

It is knowing that we are not *all* alike. When we negotiate with each other and then *define* our agreements; we meet each other's needs with *respect and honor*. Compromise has to be a *most important* part of our everyday life, in order to live in *harmony* with one another. We then face life in a *give and take* fashion, an unselfish manner. *Compromise* seeks a comfort level and the space we give to each other, provides that.

3. *CHALLENGES* ARE WHAT IS GIVEN TO ALL OF US—LIKE IT OR NOT.

It is what life is *all* about. The ways in which we *address* those challenges are what makes the *difference*. We can stamp our feet, throw temper tantrums, do whatever we choose to *engage* in, but they will *not* go away. Our *rewards* come as we begin to fight the battle *head on*, with a mature and positive attitude.

4. *COALS* CAN TURN INTO GOALS—BIG OR SMALL

We may have to walk on some *hot coals* in life, and decide whether we *choose* to turn them into *goals*. Coals can *consist* of problems, heartbreaks, challenges, and whatever else life may deal us. Goals are what *motivates us,* keeps us trying, and encourages us to *continue* on. If we look at *coals* as our *blessings,* we cultivate the desire to *strive and stretch* a bit further. This gives us the satisfaction of a job well done. Our successes will always help to *raise* our self-esteem and the *importance* of who we are. It makes us *proud* of our accomplishments. These are our *contributions* to our planet, no matter how *small* they may seem to *us*.

We need to step *quickly* on *hot* coals and rightly so—*move along*—and don't wait *too long* to become aware of the opportunities that lie in front of us. We need to make the necessary *thinking* changes from the *negative* patterns we have learned, and replace that thinking with a *positive* outlook. Let's not procrastinate and *fail* to recognize our ability to *choose.* As we set a *good* example, we help others to realize their goals, also. Don't let those goals *smolder* and become just *ashes,* like those coals. *Stay aware*—and make sure your GOALS *don't turn into dying embers.*

When we *recognize*—*control* is being used on us, we must take our *spirit* back. It has been broken, and *needs* to be healed. We strive to make the *necessary* changes to *become* ourselves again.

When we *recognize*—*challenges,* we fight to *turn* those around, and make them *work* for us—rather than *against* us. It's just about *looking* for a solution to the problem, in a different manner, than we are accustomed to doing.

When we *recognize*—*compromise* is lacking in our life, we force ourselves to examine what is *fair* and *just,* to meet some of our *own* needs. We do this with an awareness and always our *respect* for others. This is *not* a selfish taking, but a *healthy* way to live. We become *better* people and our happiness *radiates* towards others.

When we *recognize*—*hot coals,* we realize we can *alter* that fire, and step differently, instead of getting *burned.* These are *only* ashes, if we wait just a *little* while for them to *die out.* Don't forget these *coals* are part of life. What *we* do with them is up to *us.* Goals keep *our* fire burning *inside* and keep us feeling enthusiastic, happy, and alive!

I have *never* described cancer in *my* life as the *"Big C."* I also do not use it to relay a cancer diagnosis about others. *Big* denotes *power*! I for one, am *not ready* to give *all of my power away. I'm not even willing to capitalize* the word *cancer,* in my writings, if you've noticed? I won't give the *"Big C"* word, the *authority* to project an outcome and become so *definite* in telling me what the *end* results of my cancer *may* be. This is left to our *HIGHER POWER. He* decides who receives the miracles.

There are so *many* words starting with the *"Big C"* that are *more* important to keep in our vocabulary such as:

Courageous	the act of trying
Conquer	hope felt within
Caring	concern
Can	fight the fight
Comfort	doing our best to show love and devotion to our families
Communication	open our hearts to speak
Compassion	wearing another's shoes

I think I would rather *think* of these words when someone mentions the *"Big C."* How about you?

> The awesome intelligence of God is revealing the *divine solution* even as I sleep.
> —*Daily Word*—Silent Unity Magazine

> Turn your scars into stars!
> —Crystal Cathedral Calendar

> I thank you, God, that I am created to be free.
> *Daily Word*—Unity Village

14

Did You Ever Want to Live in a Bubble?—I Did

Surely God is my salvation; I will trust, and will not be afraid.

—Isaiah 12:2

Have you ever wanted to live in a bubble? *I did.*

Just think, you could be totally *protected* from everything in life.

No more emotional pain, suffering, hurts, sadness, disappointments.

My bubble will *shelter* me from everything.

Doesn't this sound great?

I am so excited!

Where will I *put* my bubble?

Where is a *good* location? I'll have to map this out.

It will be in a *real safe* place.

But, who will *live* there with me?

No one. *I am alone.*

I guess I didn't think about that?

What will give me *joy*—in my bubble?

What will give me *hope*—in my bubble?

What will I have *faith* in—in my bubble?

What will give me *pleasure*—in my bubble?

What will I have to be *grateful* for—in my bubble?

Who will give me *love*—in my bubble?

If I stay in my bubble, will my personality *change*? Will I be as happy?

I can't *see* anyone clearly anymore, because it's kind of cloudy in here.

I can't *tell* if others can see me very well.

I can't *speak* to anyone anymore, unless I shout.

I can't *hear* anyone anymore, unless they shout.

I can't *touch* anyone anymore, unless I come out of my bubble.

I can't *smell* anything much in here, except a kind of stale smell.

My bubble doesn't seem as *good* to me anymore, when I write about it.

I think my bubble will *end* my purpose in life.

I think I'll *miss* all of life.

I think my bubble will *take* life's blessings away.

I think my bubble will *shelter* me—but from everything?

I forgot about all of the *good stuff* in life that I receive when I am visible and real.

I didn't think about all of this *ending*—I'm *beginning* to feel sad.

It seems I better RE-THINK MY *BUBBLE*?

> *For everything there is a season, and a time for every matter under heaven.*
> *A time to weep, and a time to laugh.*
> —Ecclesiastes 3:1, 4

Happy are those who find wisdom.
She is a tree of life to those who lay hold of her; those who hold
her fast are called happy.

—Proverbs 3:13, 18

15

Marriage Is 50/50%—the Scorekeeper's Marks—Silence is Quiet

Marriage should be a duet—when one sings, the other claps.
—Joe Murray

Marriage is *50/50%*.

The scorekeepers gives us our *good* scores.

Silence is good because it denotes *quiet.*

This all sounds pretty *darn good*, doesn't it?

Well, I'm going to have to *break your bubble.*

Marriage is 50/50% is a *fallacy*!

Keeping score in a relationship is *deadly*!

Silence is the worst enemy of *hope*!

In a loving and secure relationship, these first three statements above *do not* exist, or are there any of these behaviors *acted* upon to support these fallacies! If we convince ourselves any of these theories will work, we will discover operating on this level will never bring staying power to any relationship. If we choose to believe the above statistics, we can expect only problems to surface and *steal* power away from each other, which only *creates* confusion in our relationships.

Those of us that have been married, even for a short time know that 50/50% is *impossible*. So, why even *attempt* the impossible? We'll only be let down, and *our* expectations *blown out of the water*! Life has too many responsibilities and changes *daily* to be able to *keep* up our end of the bargain,

Now, if we are an *unbeliever* and want to try this method of 50/50%, we will have to *keep score*. This brings us to the *marks* we will be receiving on our scoreboard. In our relationship we will have to figure out a way to do this.

We could try the system of *deposits* and *withdrawals.*

We will have to retrieve a *big* scoreboard from somewhere, as it will take up much space to keep this all straight on a *daily* basis. I guess we could put our deposits and withdrawals in a computer to keep track, but this is so *timely* every night.

Of course, if you decide to attempt this charting, one of us would have to *volunteer* to do this nightly, without an excuse for *missing* the scorekeeping.

Okay, let's begin:

Deposits will be what we *have done* that is expected of us, and that we *agreed* to do as part of our 50/50% marriage.

All of our deposits will also include the *necessary* actions taken by us to keep our marriage intact. These important qualities are what we *need* to foster in each other, and are listed below.

Honoring each other
Displaying our love
Caring and respect for each other
Recognition and awareness of each other's feelings and
    needs
Devotion shown by our loyalty to each other

The *withdrawals* will be what is *not done* and *was* expected of us.

Withdrawals will also include what has been done to *harm* our relationship.

(You may include anything else *you* wish to chart on the scoreboard.)

We will have to mark this down *every* day.

Remember, we thought it was a *good idea* to keep score!

49

It seems to me that we are putting in, taking out, checking off, changing the board so much! The *scoring* is getting all *messed* up.

I am *short* on deposits, and have *withdrawn* more by my *unloving* actions.

I am *not* in balance at all! Is this really working? Did you notice that there seem to be so many more *deposits* needed than *withdrawals*?

Keeping score is *brutal* to any relationship!

Honor, Love, Caring, Respect, Recognition, Awareness, Devotion, Loyalty does not *require* a scorekeeper.

Which one of *you* wants to be the scorekeeper? *Step up!*

Remember the old saying—the definition of Insanity.

"If you always do what you always did, you always get, what you always got."

> *In your silence, show me you feel love, you feel hope, you feel connected to me, and I will hear you speak.*
> —Joanne (Sheppard) Rybar

The last topic we need to discuss in this chapter is the *quiet time of Silence.*

A favorite passage of mine from the Bible is: *"Be still and know that I am God."* Now, in examining these *holy words,* this passage is telling us that we *need* to be quiet and listen. *Listening* is so *important.* We all know, we can be *quiet* for a few minutes and *pretend* to be listening to each other, when in fact we are just *waiting* for the opportunity and the first chance—we get to talk. This is not recognized as *good* listening skills, and is *not* recommended.

This brings us to *silence* in our relationships. Now, above I have stated that being quiet and listening is very *special* and a time of great learning if we follow the rules of *good* communication. It is very *effective,* and very *honoring* to each other.

What about the *other* type of silence, which includes making us, *wait? Waiting* can be delivered in *many* different scenarios. 1—can be a *surprise* attack, 2—can be a behavior that is *unexpected,* 3—can be an answer we did not want to *hear,* 4—can be disappointment, anxiety, sadness, and/or constant *turmoil inside of us.*

Waiting for an answer from another becomes *punishment* when it is inflicted on us *purposely.* The other knowing very well that this *form of control* becomes a *weapon* for them, to *injure* us emotionally. Now, any of you that feel so *strongly* about this type of *control,* knows full well the feelings that *swell* inside of you. If your coping strategy is to put issues on the table and sort them out, then this silence becomes *cruel and so hurtful.* It also breeds anger, resentments, frustrations and rage (if carried on long enough). Silence makes us feel *hopeless and helpless,* because it *destroys* all communication. It is also very *confusing* in a relationship because it gives off so many *mixed* messages. Without communication, we are always *surmising* and/or *guessing* at the answers. This causes great stress and is *not* a healthy way to live.

There certainly are types of personalities that have difficulty *confronting* their problems and issues. This type of personality will use *silence* to *deny* the *need* to confront. This is also *dangerous* in a relationship because without some understanding from the person we are involved with, as to what their *feelings* and *issues* are, there can be *no forgiveness* on our part. You *don't* know what you are *supposed* to forgive. You have only your *own* interpretation of the incident that took place to *create* the silence in the *first* place. We must attempt at least, to *recognize* each other's methods of coping. We only ask each other for *help* in our quest to *understand* their thoughts and feelings. This *is* an impossible task if we *live* in a *room* of silence and quiet.

> *SILENCE*—the water is still and quiet—
> no ripples—*HOW BEAUTIFUL*
> just a *little* churning now
> no, it is becoming *more* violent
> I feel the *powerful* undertow
> *Can't that be deadly?*

16

Doesn't Stuffing Sound Good

I will call upon you, O Lord; come quickly to me.
—Psalm 141:1

A term used and recognized by most of us, is the word *stuffing*. I do know that *stuffing* in a relationship breeds fear, anger, frustration, and the rage that will follow, if these emotions are not worked on and *kept* in check. This got me to thinking about stuffing my turkey on Thanksgiving. The stuffing in the turkey is *so good* and I have to make *so much* because my family loves it. I am trying to *jam* as much dressing into this big turkey as I possibly can. I have learned a few tricks along the way. I can now *stuff* an area in the side of the legs of the turkey. There is a *compartment* there that I didn't even know existed, but a very nice man informed me on how to do it. Wow! What a surprise! The only trouble is that I *still* have some dressing left to put somewhere. I guess I will have to find *another container to cook the rest of it. I just plain ran out of room!*

I was wondering if this is what happens to us when we are trying to *stuff* our *unresolved* issues and the *everyday* ones that are sure to crop up? Do we have enough room left in our bodies to *shove* down just a *little bit* more, and convince us that this *new* spot is large enough? I hope it will *protect* my anger and resentments from *surfacing*! I guess I discovered that my *storage* space in my body ran *out* of shelves! Maybe, if I was a little *taller,* I could have taken more. Maybe if I was a little *wider,* more fear, resentments, anger, and frustrations may have fit more comfortably, inside of me.

I only know the *place* I arrived at, and where this *kind* of stuffing got *me*. A place that I don't like and a *person* that I don't like. We *must* take care of our *old* wounds, as well as resolving the *new* issues that arise daily, to keep us healthy.

We *can't* keep stuffing, because like our turkey, our body is *full*—plain and simple! Our turkey will *explode* and so will *we*! When this happens something inside of us is *ever changed*! Stuffing will never be for our *best*, even though it may be *camouflaged*, and lead us to *believe* that we may be doing *quite* well. We wonder why all of a sudden, the *explosion* comes; the volcano *erupts*.

I *can't* overstuff my turkey! It won't cook *right*. It won't even *look* good. All of my dressing will be *falling out* and getting all *mixed* in with my drippings for my *special* gravy. Then, I'll have to *separate* everything; the turkey, the dressing, the juice for the gravy. This looks *messy* and seems like it is going to be a lot of *work*! I hope I can *straighten* out *my issues* before they get all *mixed* in together and continue to *create* such havoc in my life.

My goal is to learn *more* about me, and for *me* to be *open* to study *my* communication skills. Does it appear they are serving me well, or is there more work for me to do? *All of my learning will bring me to a place of peace* I am working towards, and the *serenity* I seek.

How about if we leave the stuffing for the turkey?

God grant me the Serenity to accept the things I cannot change
the Courage to change the things I can
and the Wisdom to know the difference.

—Reinhold Niebuhr

17

Let's Just Wait and See

And this is my prayer that your love may overflow more and more with knowledge and full insight.

—Philippians 1:9

Hope is the feeling you have, that the feeling you have isn't permanent.

—Jean Kerr

Waiting—to remain inactive in readiness or expectations! A position of concealment with the intent to surprise or attack!

Waiting is *not* a game anyone wants to play in a *relationship*. Certainly there are some things in life *worth* waiting for. There are our priorities that *are* important to us and *deserving* of the wait. Everyday life *dictates* our sitting in doctors' offices, encountering the lines in grocery stores and shopping malls, hoping our transportation will not be delayed, waiting for expected phone calls, guests arriving late, and on and on. Although this may be *very stressful* at times but, we will learn this does not *create* the type of *havoc* I am speaking about.

The waiting I am about to discuss *involves* anxiety, surprise, and actually can come as an attack! What are we expecting *might* happen? Are we waiting for something to be *altered* in our lives, and make it all *different*? Are we waiting for someone to *change* to suit us? Are we waiting for someone to meet *all* of our needs and then we will be *happy*? Are we waiting for that person to *step up* to the plate and take *charge* and help us, in this time of crisis? Are we waiting for the *silence* to be broken and then, I will have my *answer*?

Let's examine what *we* are waiting for. What will my life be like if I just keep this *vigil*, and *hope* that someday *my wait* will be over, and I *will* get what I need? How *long* will this take? Maybe just a week? Maybe two? Maybe a lifetime? I can't be sure. The wait may be *too* long! This seems to be a form of *torture*!

At times now, I feel *sick*. My energy seems to be *draining*. Have you felt this way? I am *confused* in trying to figure out *when* I will receive *some* kind of answer to this waiting game. I think I'd better *get moving* and *join* the universe again. I *thought* I could, but I *don't* think I will be able to——

JUST WAIT AND SEE

18

Why Did This Rage Find Me?

Then Jesus said, "Father, forgive them; for they know not what they are doing."

—Luke 23:34

Rage is capable of anything.
Rage is an attempt to explain the unexplainable.
Rage is the power to love.
Rage is the power to hate.
Rage is the power to kill.
Rage is the explosion of love and hate.
Rage is physical abuse—emotional abuse—or both.
Rage is a lack of understanding of our capabilities to act.
Rage is inexcusable.
Rage is demeaning.
Rage is disrespectful.
Rage is the destruction of love.
Rage is complicated.
Rage is the culmination of our deepest feelings.
Rage is contradictory.
Rage is fear.
Rage is a build-up of strong emotions of love.
Rage is a build-up of strong emotions of hate.
Rage is territorial.
Rage is protection.
Rage is control when there is none left.
Rage is loneliness.
Rage is sadness.
Rage is disappointment.

Rage is punishment directed towards ourselves and
   others.
Rage is helplessness.
Rage is hopelessness.
Rage seeks destruction of our soul.
Rage is Satan's work.
Rage is a place I never imagined that I would visit.

> *With a silent, heartfelt prayer, I let go and let God heal my*
> *relationships.*
> *—Daily Word*—Unity Village

> *I have the spiritual resources to meet change with success.*
> *—Daily Word*—Unity Village

> *As an ever-unfolding creation of the Creator, I am making*
> *progress every day.*
> *—Daily Word*—Unity Village

Rage is the house created for me, that I lived in for the last
   two years.

The lessons I learned from this time in my life involve so
   much,
it is difficult to *describe* and to *write* about.

Rage is *all* of these feelings that I have written, at *least* to
   me.
I so *strongly* believe today our *issues* that are *not* settled in
   our life
will certainly come back to *bite* us, at some point. It seems
   they will *find* us,
even though we *try* to hide. We may think that this will
   never happen to us.

What does your gauge of life measure concerning
   happiness, joy, and comfort?
Are you *happy*? Do you feel *joy*? Are you *comfortable* at
   home, and at work?

Is our *attitude* (most of the time) one of *gratitude*?
It is difficult to be *grateful,* when we are *unhappy.*
If we *practice* feeling grateful, it will be an enormous *aid* in
   propelling ourselves towards happiness.

Do we just *drag* along every day, and hope that life will be
   better?
Are we willing to do *something* about it?
Are we willing to stick our neck out, and *take the risk* to
   have our questions answered?
Are we willing to do some *hard* work and find *some*
   answers for a better life?
Are we willing to *remain* complacent, and just keep the
   status quo?
Are we willing to *compromise* ourselves, and/or stay *stuck*
   in this place of unhappiness?

Where will our unanswered issues *reside*?
Where will our feelings that are unresolved *hide*?
Where will our resentments *live*?
Where will our anger *visit*, when we least expect it?
These are the questions that I have had to ask *myself.*

First the *fear* sets in *slowly* and *cunningly.* Anger *follows* and
   is sure to
create more *frustration* and *anxiety.* When our frustration
   level hits
its peak and *explodes,* rage is *waiting,* not far behind.

I was *not* able to decipher, in experiencing *all* of these
      range of emotions, how to
save myself from the *rage.* Satan will take you *there*—if *you*
      allow it.

DON'T GO THERE—IT IS SATAN'S PLACE AND A PIT OF HELL

*Pray for one another, so that you may be healed. The prayer
of the believer is powerful and effective.*

—James 5:16

19

My Lonely Letter

A critic is a man who knows the way but can't drive the car.
                                                    —Kenneth Tynan

Thought and learning are of small value unless translated into action.
                                                    —Wang Ming

Have you ever written a letter to someone, put your whole heart in it, and been turned down?

Turned down meaning experiencing—sadness, sorrow, that crushing feeling, tears, heartache.

"What does *turned down* mean in a relationship with another?" you ask. Well, *think of it this way.*

Turned is defined as rotating, sudden or brief disorder of body and/or spirit, a spell of nervous shock, rejected.

Down is defined as to/or towards the lower end or bottom, depressed, dejected, defeated.

This would be quite a *range* of emotions happening *all* at one time! When we experience this *enormous* turmoil, what is this doing to us? What is happening to our bodies? This is terrible! *I'm scared! Sadness* is greeting me on one side. The *pain* expresses itself on another. *Sorrow* lies waiting at the next turn. I have a *crushing* feeling lying face down on the *bottom* of some pit. My heart is *aching.* It really hurts! Could I really die of a *broken* heart? I'm going to *cry.* All of this tossing me *up, down* and *sideways* makes me feel *confused*! I am *spinning* out of control! I want you to *stop*! I feel *this* in my *whole* body, and my head is *pounding.* Don't my *tears* show you my *hurt*?

Well, I wrote a letter many years ago to my mother. I *poured* out my heart about my feelings and the caring I had for her, and I was *turned down.* We had been struggling with our relationship for a couple of years, and I felt that this letter may help to explain my feelings and get us *back on track* with each other. My mother shared this with my sister, and that *gave* them permission to make fun of my letter and me. *Imagine* my shock when I realized that this is what my mom had done! I can still remember that day and the *profound* impact it had on me. *I think it changed my life!*

I recently wrote to another person about my *accomplishments* and made a *list* of what I had done to *help* make our relationship *better.* I was criticized again, for this writing *not* matching up to their expectations. I had to sit there with this list of mine and listen, as it was *picked* apart, to have *that* person's *comfort* be the most *important* criteria.

I started to cry and scream that all of what I wrote was *truthful.*

I worked very hard to *accomplish* these agreements to make life better for us.

I felt it would be a *stepping stone* for both of us to *repair* the damage in this relationship.

What I had accomplished *was good,* but I was told—"not quite *Good Enough."* There were tiny remarks of questioning as we moved from line to line on my list, making my accomplishments seem so *small a contribution!*

Then it *happened!* Came the deep *sadness,* the *sorrow,* that *crushing* feeling, the *tears* and the *heartache.* It was that *same* feeling I had so many years ago on that day that I was made to feel *so unimportant.*

Today, I know my mother's thinking was not clear, and her head was foggy, I'm sure, with all the alcohol. Nevertheless, these situations hurt *beyond* description. We have to *attempt* to understand what the other person is experiencing at this time, and hopefully this will *help* to *heal* our hurt.

These *new* agreements with this person were *so from my heart*! It was such a struggle for me to *complete* all of these statements that I had *promised* to do, and in fact *DID DO*!

Why weren't my efforts *appreciated*?

Why wasn't I *recognized* for what I had done?

Why weren't my feelings *validated*?

Why were my accomplishments *cast aside*?

Why do I have to be *criticized* for not doing enough?

I made the connection from all of my tears *today* to that letter of many years ago. It was a letter to attempt to make my life better with my mom. Her alcoholism of so many years certainly had *affected* me. I just wanted to explain that I was more understanding of *her* pain. I don't think that was *funny*?

This Memorial weekend of sadness *dictated* to me that I ask myself to *dig* deep down inside to that *dark* place, and find out where *all* of this sadness and sorrow is coming from. Hopefully, this will at least bring understanding and knowledge to try to *heal* this *ugly* spot that now seems *etched* into my heart.

Why *were* my efforts and my accomplishments met today with just criticism and *turned down*? I am working hard to learn more and *move* forward to *gain* more knowledge, but this is *all* I know today. It will just take a *little* more time. Be *patient with me* and understand *my* struggles. Gaining more knowledge is a *life-long* job, and I have *chosen* to learn.

My letter was *lonely* many years ago because it was met with ridicule, torn apart, and *turned down* for the enjoyment of someone else's pleasure. No one would *defend* that letter of many years ago.

Not Even Me!

My writing and *list* of accomplishments seem *lonely* today.

They are sitting all by *themselves* on my kitchen table.

It is *crumbled* and *torn* now, because of my *anger.* They seem to be worth *nothing.*

But then I stopped! I looked at it. *I cried.* I looked at what I had written and knew it was my *TRUTH.* I did these things, I wrote.

My barometer that I had used to gauge my accomplishments and myself through my life were *off kilter. My* thinking was lopsided, *turned around* and *upside down.* I should have given *myself* credit so many years ago for what I was trying to accomplish in an attempt to make my relationship with my mom a better one. Today, I am working hard to make *me* a better person and I want to *share* my learning with those closest to me. I don't *need* someone else to *tell* me what I know is *my truth*?

I don't want my *new* accomplishments to lay *lonely* on that table.

I *won't allow* this to happen a *second time!*

Who will defend them? *I WILL.*

20

Please—Accommodate Me

A happy memory never wears out.

—Libbie Fudim

I think most of us are familiar with needing to be accommodated at times. It could be an accommodation at a hotel, carrying our luggage, asking a question. I guess we could really describe—*to accommodate*—by saying it is an *interest* and a *concern* for another. If we feel taken care of, helped and kindness shown, it *does* make us happy.

We would agree then that accommodating is: willingness, thoughtfulness, cooperation and a desire to share in another's happiness. It becomes apparent when practicing this way of life, we *bring* pleasure into the lives of others.

In a *relationship,* we must remember that accommodating is a *twofold* proposition. This meaning we are *not* always the one to be *doing* the work, but certainly expecting the other person to be *willing* to reciprocate. We may find ourselves in a relationship realizing we are the *one* always putting forth the effort. One-sided accommodating becomes *selfish* and *removes* the give and take. If we continue giving, in an attempt to make the other person happy, without loving action on their part, the *deal is off!* In this type of relationship comes resentment, anger, and then falls into the category of feeling *used* and *abused.*

This brings us to the difference between accommodating and *catering.* The word that *must* always be kept in mind and sometimes we may forget, is *compromise.* Compromise *shows* love and affection and most importantly thoughtfulness. Let's not find ourselves being accommodated constantly and turn that caring action from others into a *selfish* taking for our own *comfort*. There is a thin line here and it isn't something to be *taken* for granted. Boundaries in our relationships are *sacred*, not to be crossed over, and with knowing the importance of our need to compromise and consider each other in *all* our affairs.

Let's pretend we are building a stairway. Attempt to visualize these scenarios. We will fill in our *own* words that will make us understand just what we *need* to do, and come to see a clearer picture of what accommodating means.

Step 1—Willingness is the first step on our stairway to reach another. Willingness tells *much* about us. It tells how far we will *extend* ourselves for someone else. Putting forth *effort* is all that is asked of us.

Step 2—Thoughtfulness, our second step, is our caring and concern for others. Thoughtfulness is not blind-sited. It is doing something to be of help to another. *True* concern is all that is required.

Step 3—Cooperation follows just ahead of us, rather than behind us. We can't make it to the top without it, as we strive to *complete* our climb. Cooperation is a very *powerful act*—not just a word—but also an *action,* as *is* the rest of our stairs. To cooperate means giving of ourselves without wanting a *return.* With cooperation comes *no* complaints. Our clock must have *no* hands, as we generously give our time to *create* our *special* time clock. A *caring* clock is all that is necessary.

Step 4—Desire wants something and goes about the job of *doing* what it takes to accomplish that goal. How much do we *desire* to make someone else happy? Bad enough to do some *work* and put *forth* the effort necessary to *show* our good intentions? If the answer to this question is *yes,* you have just stepped foot on the *top* of the stairs.

I think the *top* is called the *landing* because it actually means we *have* landed! *I'm here!* I succeeded in *proving* my devotion. Was that climb as *difficult* as you thought, or was there pleasure in it *for you* also, as you watched the happiness *you* created—*by accommodating me?*

21

Loyalty—a Sacred and Holy Word

Do not let loyalty and faithfulness forsake you; bind them around your neck, write them on the tablet of your heart.
—Proverbs 3:3

What is the definition of loyalty?

The dictionary says it is *faithfulness.*
It is *constant.*
It is adhering to *commitments and obligations.*
It is *devotion* to one another.
It is *support* for each other.
It is a *sense* of duty.
Wow! That sure is a *great* many examples for one word!

I was thinking about this word, and decided to check it out in the dictionary, because it struck me as being such an *important* word. We don't hear it used much in conversation, and yet it envelops *so* much of who we are. It determines our many *actions* and *reactions* in dealing with family, friends, and everyone around us.

In making a list of the words we should hold *sacred* and *holy,* I'm sure you would *agree,* they would include: Loyalty, Truth, Honor, Honesty, Love, and Respect. All of these words have such a *profound* effect on us through *all* of life. When we acknowledge these *holy* words and act accordingly, we *mold* who we become. Our *choices* throughout life are then touched in a *holy way.*

Our loyalty may be tested at times, more times than we may want to *recognize.* We show our loyalty to others when

68

we have the *courage* to *announce* that we see an *injustice* being done, and *defending* what we know is right.

There are *many* other situations that come up allowing us the opportunity to show our *devotion* to others. Loyalty *is* devotion. It is our *dedication* to stand *behind* each other, when the need is there.

In *analyzing* this word, I think it is *all* of these definitions that I found in my dictionary.

It is remaining *faithful*.

It is being *constant*.

It is taking our *commitments* and *obligations* seriously.

It is a *devotion* that is recognizable and visible.

It is our continued *support* of others.

It is that feeling of *duty* owed to others that we choose to act upon.

We have all probably experienced the *effects* of betrayal by someone close to us, at sometime in our life. It may have been the *loss* of loyalty of someone *very important*. Maybe, we were shocked and disappointed! We put our *trust* in them and an *expectation* that they would *defend* us, *if need be*. So what *happened* at a time when I needed you? I *knew* in my heart that I had *earned* your loyalty and I am *deserving* of it.

WHERE DID YOU GO? I AM STANDING ALONE.

22

I Cried Today

*Be kind to one another, tenderhearted, forgiving one another,
as God in Christ has forgiven you.
Therefore be imitators of God, as beloved children, and live in
love, as Christ loved us.*

—Ephesians 4:32—5:1–2

I CRIED TODAY because of *all* of my blessings shown to me
on Mother's Day.

I CRIED TODAY because I *honor* and *applaud* my mother.

I CRIED TODAY because I was *waiting* for the prognosis of a
cancer diagnosis.

I CRIED TODAY because I had to face life in that realistic
way that *can* and *does* slap you in the face.

I CRIED TODAY because I was *mourning* my losses throughout my life.

I CRIED TODAY because I thought of my mother and all of
her hardships.

I CRIED TODAY because we were blessed with *no* chemo-
therapy treatments in this diagnosis of cancer.

I CRIED TODAY because I had *hurt* feelings on Mother's
Day.

I CRIED TODAY because I *wanted* to feel.

I CRIED TODAY because I have caused my *family* pain.

I CRIED TODAY because I am *blessed.*

I CRIED TODAY because I have seven months of *sobriety.*

I CRIED TODAY because I thought of my mom and *mourned*
her loss.

I CRIED TODAY because I am *humbled.*

I CRIED TODAY because I am remembering my mother-in-law who taught me so much and the *gratitude* I feel for our relationship.

I CRIED TODAY because I have *beautiful* grandchildren and they have wonderful parents.

I CRIED TODAY because my baggage of life has been *heavy.*

I CRIED TODAY because I had to grow up *too* fast.

I CRIED TODAY because I thought of my mom's *accomplishments* in the last ten years of her life.

I CRIED TODAY because I have *freed* myself of judgment.

I CRIED TODAY because I am healing and I *can* feel it.

I CRIED TODAY because I have given myself *permission* to just tell the facts of my life.

I CRIED TODAY because my responsibilities as a child were *unfair.*

I CRIED TODAY because I have worked to make my baggage lighter and *not* weigh me down.

I CRIED TODAY because I *understand* my dad better.

I CRIED TODAY because of all I have *witnessed* in my young life.

I CRIED TODAY because I *miss* my mother and my mother-in-law.

I CRIED TODAY because I just *celebrated* twenty-six years of being a cancer survivor.

I CRIED TODAY because I am able to get in touch with my *deepest* feelings.

I CRIED TODAY because I am *not* afraid anymore.

I CRIED TODAY because I don't have to *abuse* alcohol to get to my deepest feelings.

I CRIED TODAY because I appreciate my dad's strengths and *forgive* his weaknesses.

I CRIED TODAY because I *want* my security back.

I CRIED TODAY because so many of my prayers have been *answered.*

I CRIED TODAY because *St. Anthony* is taking care of me
   now.

   The wind blows where it chooses, and you hear the sound of
   it, but you do not know where it comes from, or where it goes.
   So it is with everyone who is born of the Spirit.
                                                        —John 3:8

   Divine love soothes my heart and uplifts my spirits.
                              Daily Word—Unity Village

23

Did You Ever Wonder Why?

And a harvest of righteousness is sown in peace for those who make peace.

—James 3:18

DID YOU EVER WONDER WHY you want to *stop* the world and get off?

DID YOU EVER WONDER WHY your life *changed* after a cancer diagnosis?

DID YOU EVER WONDER WHY you are *hurting* from a cancer diagnosis?

DID YOU EVER WONDER WHY other's lives are so busy and yours seems to be so *quiet*?

DID YOU EVER WONDER WHY everyone is rushing around doing so many things, and you are *pushing* yourself to get dressed?

DID YOU EVER WONDER WHY people are talking and laughing and you are sad and *focused* on cancer?

DID YOU EVER WONDER WHY you are *not* interested right now in anything anyone else is talking about?

DID YOU EVER WONDER WHY others don't seem to *understand* your sadness?

DID YOU EVER WONDER WHY people are trying to keep you moving and you just *slowed* down?

DID YOU EVER WONDER WHY you seem to be thinking of what life is really about and want to *tell* it to someone?

DID YOU EVER WONDER WHY you seem *more* sensitive today?

DID YOU EVER WONDER WHY you are *searching* for more joy?

DID YOU EVER WONDER WHY you want people to *understand* you better now?

DID YOU EVER WONDER WHY you *retreat* to your life's old memories?

DID YOU EVER WONDER WHY as a mom, you are thinking about when your children were *babies*?

DID YOU EVER WONDER WHY you are *thinking* of their growing up years?

DID YOU EVER WONDER WHY you *look* at life with a deeper meaning than before?

DID YOU EVER WONDER WHY you sometimes want to *shout* things out?

DID YOU EVER WONDER WHY you *expect* yourself to examine your faults?

DID YOU EVER WONDER WHY you feel a *need* to tell your children and your grandchildren the story of your life?

DID YOU EVER WONDER WHY you *want* others to understand why you've lived the life you have lived?

DID YOU EVER WONDER WHY you want to state what you have been taught and how you *arrived* at this place in life?

DID YOU EVER WONDER WHY you want to *run* away?

DID YOU EVER WONDER WHY there are so many *more* stars now in the sky at night?

DID YOU EVER WONDER WHY your expectations of yourself seem to *push* you to make restitution to others?

DID YOU EVER WONDER WHY your feelings seem to be hurt *more* easily?

DID YOU EVER WONDER WHY the trees seem to be *growing* so big?

DID YOU EVER WONDER WHY those resentments harbored deep inside want to be *cleansed*?

DID YOU EVER WONDER WHY you want to take *long* rides in the country?

DID YOU EVER WONDER WHY it is sometimes *difficult* to fight depression?

DID YOU EVER WONDER WHY you *question* your purpose here on earth?

DID YOU EVER WONDER WHY you *think* more of the after-life?

DID YOU EVER WONDER WHY you ask yourself if you *succeeded* in completing your purpose?

DID YOU EVER WONDER WHY you want to *seek* out a peaceful place by the sea?

DID YOU EVER WONDER WHY you want to tell more about your *intent* concerning your actions?

DID YOU EVER WONDER WHY you feel that pull and the strength to be positive and *not* negative?

DID YOU EVER WONDER WHY you are filled with so much more *love* in your soul?

DID YOU EVER WONDER WHY?

24

My Precious Traveling Suitcase Got Old

Now is the acceptable time.

—Corinthians 6:2

My *old* suitcase holds my precious items that I love. I've hung on to this *old* trunk of mine because it made me *feel good* to possess all of my special treasures. Oh, I could never part with this great stuff that has been a part of me for so long! Everything seems too *good* in that old suitcase I have traveled with, for so many years.

Then one day, my lock *broke* and it popped open. Everything started falling out! I had left it lying on its side. Everything was getting all *messed in* with everything else! I had kept my treasures so *neat* and *tidy* all these years. I shouldn't have been so *careless*. I'm sure it was right side up when I left it *tucked* away so *carefully,* in my closet.

I began to *compare* my suitcase to my life. That's what happened to me! The same thing that *occurred* in my suitcase! As I had to straighten out all of my treasures in that *old* trunk, I had to begin my work and the *exact* same process in my head. I had to *start* sorting.

I noticed something very strange, as I began this *process.* My treasures and the favorite items I *clung* to so tightly are *outdated.* I can't wear them anymore. I won't look good and especially, I won't *feel* good. Some don't *even* fit! I can't *wear* those same old hats that I had worn as a young person. I can't *adorn* myself with that outfit, which is now *moldy.* I think I'll even *stink* in this covering on my body. This will make me *sad* and *self-conscious.* People won't want to be

76

around me anymore. *I* will be *outdated.* I'd better dress in something better. My *old* baggage doesn't look like treasures, as I *examine* them more closely.

I think this is similar to our baggage we *drag* with us, from our childhood years. We all bring at least *one* suitcase with us. Of course, some of us bring *much* more. I need to share what is inside this *old* piece of luggage! It feels *heavy.* It is *weighing* me down today. This baggage of *mine* is what constitutes my thoughts, my actions and reactions because of my life's experiences. It stands to reason, that what I know will most likely *dictate* the life I choose for myself, *if I allow it.* I think maybe, it is time to *quit* pointing our finger and making excuses for that house, that school, that person, or whatever else did not bring us happiness and safety. We need to *stop blaming* and *share* with one another to explain, and hopefully gain understanding about what we were *taught* and what we *learned,* by example. I ask for *your* acceptance of me, concerning my life and the circumstances I lived under. I do have a *choice* today, whether to make my *old learning* a *permanent* dwelling place in my head. I could just say that these thoughts were *only visiting,* as I did when I went on a vacation with that *old trunk* of mine. I can *decide* to change course and move on, so as my *beliefs of old* could *reside* in a better place?

Why did I *hang on* to all of this *old* thinking? I will have to *let go* of that which is *binding* me to *old thoughts,* and *proclaims* to be treasures, which I have *packed* in my head. These beliefs do *not* serve me well anymore and certainly gives me no joy. I know this will be a *tough* one! All of this is what I have been *familiar* with throughout my young life, and probably *most* of my adult life. This is the baggage I have carried around for a *long* time, and actually, *I like it.* It makes me *comfortable.*

I wonder if I could have *brain surgery* on my thinking?

We have surgery to make our bodies *healthy* and *strong* again. I guess I *can't* have surgery on my head, so what will I do about *my thinking*? I will have to find my *own* way to feel better, and *proceed to change* my mental thoughts and behaviors. This sure feels like *major surgery* to me! It seems this operation is pretty *scary*! I've never tried *changing* my brain, and carrying around a *new* one. I know they use pretty regular-looking instruments in surgery, on our bodies (I've seen them). I think there are *tools* we can use to give us insight into what we are trying to accomplish. This would sure be helpful. There are *self-help* books. How about some helpful *videos* that I know are available? We could talk to a professional counselor, who would certainly *guide us* in the right direction.

I'm *not* a surgeon, but I am willing to try to *operate* on a different level.

I do know that we must be *gentle* with ourselves, just as we were with our *old* suitcase that we *loved* and *clung* to, for so many years now. We *can't* just all of a sudden *change* everything! We must start this process *slowly*, but remember to be *consistent* in our efforts to *forge* ahead. We have *traveled* with this *same* brain for our entire life. We thought we were *storing* our thoughts in a *safe* place in our head, as I thought that *old trunk* was also safe. I wonder if our *brain* gets *moldy*? I guess we can *allow* it to become *old* and *outdated*.

Surgery *hurts* for most of us. Don't expect *instant* recovery, as we do not expect this with our *physical* mending. I am going to do it just *one day at a time*, and try to be the best that I can be, in my *new* endeavor. I *will* be patient. I will work hard, anticipate, and *believe* that good will follow. Let's acknowledge our accomplishments and be *proud* of them, as this gives us our *willingness* to continue. Day-by-day, we will feel our *heads healing* and know the *power* we have to *change* our thinking. I will pursue my *new* learning to change my *old* thinking, because I decided it was *worth* it!

I think I'll plan to go on a *new* journey. This venture will *renew* me and make me happier. I think I will *learn* more about myself and gain the knowledge I need to make my *new* path in life a better one. I'll have to *plan*. I'll have to *prepare*. I am going to *chart* my course. I think I'll want to go on a *longer* trip than my childhood years took me. I might just *stay there* and live in this *new* place that I will *prepare* for myself. Wow, I feel *better* already! This feels like a *vacation* spot, compared to the *old life* that I previously lived. How come I didn't think of this before? I don't have to *carry* around that *old* stuff in my head anymore, if I don't want to. I didn't *know* I could get *rid* of it, if I just worked at *changing* my thoughts and behaviors. What a *surprise*!

That *old* trunk is *torn and tattered*. I didn't really want to *admit* that it is *falling apart*—because, I was *so attached* to it. No wonder the lock *broke*! I've carried it *too* long. I think I'll even buy myself a *new* one. It will be a smaller suitcase. It seems I have *disposed* of so much of the *old* and replaced it with the *new*, that I don't need as *much room* for my *new* trip. It is surprising how much *less space* is needed with my new *treasures* that I have now *packed* into my *head* and my *heart*. I must remember to bring only what is *worthwhile* and most *important* to me now. I will *let go* and *let God* help me pack for this *longer* journey I am about to embark on. My *new* suitcase feels like a *feather*, compared to that *old* trunk. It reminds me of a bird in *flight*. You know, the one *trying* to find a *good* spot to *land*.

Do you have a precious *old* suitcase you want to get rid of?

25

Emotional Integrity—What's That Mean?

Emotions—an active state of consciousness in which joy, sorrow, fear, hate, or the like is experienced, any strong agitation of the feeling actuated by these experiences usually accompanied by certain psychological changes, an increased heartbeat, powerful emotions shown of joy, sorrow, fear, hate, frustration, affected or determined by emotion rather than reason.

Integrity—soundness of, or adherence to, moral principle and character uprightness, honesty, whole, entire.

These added definitions come from the *Webster's Medical Dictionary:* Emotional—psychic and physical reaction (anger or fear) that prepare the body for immediate vigorous action.

Integrity—an *unimpaired* condition of brain function.

Integrity is a word often used in business; our discussion of others; our description of someone; and always seems to fall into a category with a slant towards a *positive* side. We use the word integrity to describe (usually a positive statement) someone we have met or had dealings with in some shape or form. Integrity seems to always represent a person who is *worth* knowing. It seems a *good* thing.

Basically, integrity involves caring about the welfare of others. We act on our concern, for an effect that our actions will be with *good* judgment. What about when we place the word *emotional* in front of *integrity*? What have we then *added* into the *mix* of *two* words?

I heard the term *emotional integrity* used one day. It

struck me like a ton of bricks! I had *never* really thought *much* about it? This is an *action* we perform *daily*. The word emotional *involves* our *physical* being and *state* of mind. This means that we can actually be *responsible* in *creating* others' thinking and cause an effect on their bodies! I didn't know it involved so *much* of *me*, and so *much* of *you*.

How powerful is this? This was a *scary* lesson for me to acknowledge. I *hold* in my *head* and *behavior*, this kind of *power* over another person? Wow! I'd better be *careful* of the way I use these *tools* that I possess. I think they become *power* tools and will *react* so quickly on others, it would surprise me! I do know my words and actions can so *profoundly* affect another. They can *leave* a *mark* on someone's heart and soul for a *lifetime*. I sure don't want to have to *own up* to doing this to someone!

From all of the definitions stated above, there is quite a bit to be *discovered* and *questioned* about our emotional integrity? I am going to have to *examine* myself and realize the effect of my actions, if and when, I *decide* to *proceed* with a *lack of* concern for another. This means that I can *change* someone else's thinking, and cause them *unrest*, along with creating *havoc* on their physical well-being, as well!

I received this card from my very dear friend, after her visit to Ireland. The *good* news is that you *don't* have to be Irish to *follow* your heart. I thought it might be *suitable* here to connect with—what *emotional integrity* requires from us.

On this card, is the Claddagh Symbol, an age-old Irish emblem of faith and affection. It is a very *beautiful* emblem. This is a symbol of the working class people of Ireland that served the well-to-do. The message on this card is a lesson worth looking at, and a great example of a *lifestyle* we could all *cherish*, regardless of the category our type of work places us in.

There are three *basic* symbols: Gentle *Hands* are clasped

in *Friendship*. A *Heart* displayed in *Love*. The *Crown* shown as the symbol of our *Loyalty* to our fellow man.

If we followed this *path*, respecting the significance of these symbols, *and chose* to act on them in our *daily* life, it seems we wouldn't have to *worry* much about our *emotional integrity* remaining intact. What do you think?

> *Every day is lost in which we do not learn something useful. Man has no nobler or more valuable possession than time.*
> —Ludwig van Beethoven

> *Put things in order, listen to my appeal, agree with one another, live in peace; and the God of love and peace will be with you. Greet one another with a holy kiss.*
> —2 Corinthians 13:11–12

26

Yeah! We're Sisters

People enter our lives
for a reason
for a season or
for a lifetime.

I felt something was *missing* in my book, so I talked it over with St. Anthony one morning during prayer and meditation time. It was a chapter *not* written yet? Then he gave me *that* nudge again, and *clued* me in. I realized it was about *sisters*! I needed to write about these *wonderful* women in my life, and what they have *meant* to me.

I write this chapter with the greatest humility realizing the *gifts* that have been given to me, *because of them.*

What is a sister?
A sister is—listening, an ear without judgment
A sister is—acceptance, claiming us for who we are
A sister is—love, unceasing
A sister is—patient, remaining on watch, and guiding with love
A sister is—faith, when ours is wavering
A sister is—hope, when the waters are the darkest
A sister is—kindness, when the world feels so unkind
A sister is—action, not waiting to be told what to do, just doing it
A sister is—encouragement, always standing behind you
A sister is—advice, when asked, to direct us to a better way

A sister is—gentle, when we are so fragile

A sister is—constant, letting us know her strength is there
to borrow

A sister is—loyal, trusting our secrets, never to be violated

A sister is—honor, the respect always shown to each other

> *Shared humor soothes our hearts and connects us in a
> moment of gladness.*
> —*Daily Word*—Unity Village

I have three biological sisters whom I am *blessed* with,
but my journey has been graced with other sisters. I claim
them as sisters too, because they have left their *indelible*
mark on my *heart* and *soul*.

My biological sister *Ruthie* and I have remained very
close to each other, especially over the last ten years. We
work very hard to keep our relationship loving and constant
in all matters. I continue to learn from Ruthie, as she is a
great teacher of life. She has a steadfast faith in God and St.
Jude Thaddeus, which at times puts me to shame. She continues to be a *believer* in a sometimes-unbelievable world.
She has an undying *devotion* to those she loves, and it is always *visible.* Ruthie is one of the most *honest* and *just* people
I will ever meet. Her resilience to life continues to *amaze* me,
as I watch her meet one challenge after another and move
forward, no matter the cost. Because of a very intense and
sad childhood, we now have been able to open the door to
what *did* happen to all four of us and hopefully, heal from
this time. Ruthie and I have done our healing through love,
honor, honest communication, devotion to each other and
humor. Yes, humor we know is one of the *greatest* healers. I
am truly *blessed* and *privileged* to call her my sister and have
her in my life. Ruthie gave me a plaque many years ago, and

it reads——*CHANCE MADE US SISTERS, HEARTS MADE US FRIENDS.* I *treasure* this.

I list my *adopted* sisters below, but *not in the order of their importance.* These *short* descriptions are only a *small* part of our *sharing* as sisters. It would take *another* book to give you all of the details of our relationship and what has been given to me, *by all of them.*

Janet (Mettie) LaFaive

Jan is my sister of fifty-seven years. We were raised together. I was *privileged* to be a part of her mother, dad, and brother for many years also. Her parents taught me so much about life and showed kindness during my young years, when many others did not. Jan is a very *loving* and *generous* person. She has overcome hurdle after hurdle in her lifetime, but still continues to remain positive, despite whatever comes her way. Jan will always go the *extra mile* to help anyone. She has remained very *close* to me over the years. We have been through births, deaths, joys, sorrows, and *all* of life's challenges together.

I certainly know that whenever there is *need* to share, she is *always* just a phone call away.

Carmen (Santiago) Sluder

Carmen and I met when I was thirteen years old. Now, Carmen says that I had a *ponytail* when she first met me. I say, *"No"!* This debate has gone on now for fifty years. We had our first and second babies together on the same day, same year, same hospital, same doctor. I guess you could call us *really* close friends! We were moving right after my mastectomy, and Carmen came every night from working a full day herself, to help with our move and grace us with her decorating talents. She must have been *so* tired! I hope I have told her what that time she gave so *generously*, meant to me. She made my recovery so much easier. Carmen is a very *unique* and *wise* woman. She *couldn't* be replaced!

Sharon (Rybarski) Hill

Sharon is my sister-in-law who has remained *close* to me and her brother for over forty-six years now. Sharon was just a *little* person when I first met her. Her dad was ill and passed away shortly after I came into the family. She was to lose her mother at a very young age also. I always felt a *mother* to her in many ways and always want to keep her *close* to me.

Noreen (Thorpe) Bidigare

Noreen and I had our third babies on the same day, same year, same hospital, same doctor. In the 1950s, bed space being so crowded, Noreen was *lucky* enough to share the labor room with me, *after* the birth of her number three child. No sleep for Noreen that morning! We became friends and our daughters will celebrate their forty-third birthday in September of this year. If you are fortunate enough to have Noreen as your friend, you will be guided by a person who fills *all* of the requirements listed, as to my definition of what a sister is? She is *humble,* but we *had* to name her Saint Noreen.

Rosemary (Vitale) Kaslly

Rosemary left a *mark* on my soul, because of her *goodness*. She steps *up* when the chips are *down*. She always knows what to do to help when times are rough. She gives *comfort* to all her friends. Rosemary and I had gone on retreat from our church together for many years. One year as we were getting ready to go, my youngest, then about twelve years old, asked why we go on retreat? I answered, "To become a better person." Dianna then asked, "Why does Mrs. Kaslly have to go?" *(No mention of me.)*

Pauline (Cardella) Coury

Pauline is a part of our circle of friendship also. Pauline now resides permanently in Florida. Pauline is a very *honest* and a *straightforward* person. She *helps* you cut through any garbage that you may want to *hang* on to. What a *great* contribution, and a *plus* in anyone's life. She shortens your pain. *I miss her.*

Margaret Mary (Jentzen) Roach

Margaret Mary is my up north friend. I always picture us there, as we spent so much time together in the North Country raising our kids. Margaret Mary is a *loyal* friend. If you are in need, just pick up the phone, or *don't* pick it up, and she is there. Margaret Mary will travel however many miles it takes to *reach* a friend. She never tires of helping others. She spent the first few weeks after my mastectomy with me, in the North Country. I had to do my therapy on my arm daily, as this is so *important* after a mastectomy. Margaret

Mary *marked* the wall, as I continued to stretch those muscles in my arm, and tried to reach the next plateau. She is a tough! Don't think you're going to be *slacking off* the next day, just because you thought you did pretty good the day before!

I thank her for her *caring,* and the *love* she gave to my physical therapy time. Margaret Mary does *not* have a biological sister. Although, the truth of the matter is that you would not know which one of her women friends were *not* her biological sisters because of her devotion to them.

Marie Duffy

Marie is a therapist and one of the *best* in her profession. We have been friends now for thirty-four years. Marie lives out of state, in that beautiful setting in the East called Massachusetts. We stay close to each other, as we have shared so much over the years from births, deaths, joys, and sorrows.

We were on vacation together one summer, and Marie said that we were going to *climb a mountain* the next morning. I got up and *prepared* to climb. I showered, did my hair, applied my makeup, and put on earrings to *match* my outfit. The *only* smart thing I did was to wear *my walking shoes.* I didn't know she really *meant* a mountain! We made it to the top. Of course, I didn't look *quite* as good as when I started out. My *motto* became—*Make* a Mountain out of a Mole Hill!

Marie and I have discussed everything imaginable over the years and solved *all* of the world's problems together. Even though Marie may be your really good friend, when she puts on her *therapy hat*—(as I call it)—don't think you're going to *get a break* from what she thinks you *need* to hear! Marie is *special* in my life. She is loving, honest, gentle, and caring about others. Marie lost her only sister at the young age of thirty-five. She said that God had chosen to take her sister, but did give her a replacement, and *I was it*! How *moved* I was to receive one of the *greatest* compliments in *my* life.

Carol Gutt

I met Carol through Marie. Carol is a person who *cuts* to the chase. You won't have to sit around a *long* time and try to figure out what Carol is trying to communicate. We have *shared* the fact that both of us have been diagnosed with breast cancer. We both continue to hang in there and stay well. Our *bond* with each other has been *created* because of this disease. Carol is an *anchor* in life when others need to *feel* safe. She sure is a *good* sister.

Mary (Orrico) Treiber

Mary is my sister Ruthie's dear friend. They have been friends for many years now. Mary is the kind of a friend whom *everyone* needs. Mary is able to state what is really going on in your situation with frankness, honesty, but backed with love. I have always told Ruthie that Mary can say more to her and *get away with it*, better than any one else. This, of course, is not a bad thing, because it makes us *sit up* and take notice of the truth *very* quickly. Mary is always ready at the drop of a hat to support you. It could be a meeting, talking, a movie, dinner, whatever is needed to help *you* feel better. I have spent much time with Mary over these last five years, and *welcome* her friendship. She sure is deserving of the sister name.

Jeanie (Carroll) Collins

Jeanie also came into my life because of my sister, Ruthie. Jeanie is the type of friend that if you were able to choose only *one* friend, she would be it. She remains *constant* through your everyday life. She is a tremendous listener and always adds words of *comfort,* no matter the situation you are facing. Jeanie is always available, however tired *she* may be. She continues to support Ruthie with the *grace* and *ease* of her spirit. I have been lucky that she became Ruthie's friend, and now I get to *claim her* as my sister too.

Jenny (Rallo) Gjeldum

I met Jenny twenty years ago, through our church. You know the kind of person you *connect* with right away? That's how it was with Jenny and I. She is an extremely *compassionate* person and always looks for the *good* in others and ways to help them. Jenny is a *great* listener. She uses her ability to understand others, based on a *deep* spiritual level. She won't take credit for her *many* talents, because she remains a very *humble* person. I will *continue* to listen to her, as she is *full* of wisdom.

Nora (Duffy) Devlin

I first met Nora and her family in the North Country, when they were vacationing. *This* most important person in my life is my *sister and a surrogate mother.* Nora has been my replacement for a mother, because she is a few years older than I. She is a fine *example* of what a mother should be to her children. She stands by them through *thick and thin.* I have had many talks with Nora over the years, and sharing comes *easily* for her. I am *grateful* to have her in my life all these years and will *place* her just above the sister level, as mothers sit on a *little* different throne. Nora sits up *high*!

Dorothy (Walkley) Hanna

I met Dorothy rather by mistake. By this, I mean that her husband, Bob, worked with Ron, my husband, for many years. They were included in our guest list for our son and daughter-in-law's wedding. Dorothy was *reluctant* to come, as she really knew no one who was attending the wedding. She decided to come anyway. This was my first introduction to her. From that day on, we became close friends. It is sometimes strange when two men are close for so many years and then comes a meeting of two women, and a *bond* is formed.

Dorothy and Bob included us in wonderful days in Ann Arbor to participate in the University of Michigan football games. We have done this now every year, for many years. Dorothy is the oldest of ten children. She remains a *sister* and a *nurturer* to all of her siblings. She is a very *spiritual* person and has comforted me many times by her *presence* in my life. She stays close to me in good thoughts I feel coming my way. As she pops in and out of my head, a card is waiting for me in my mailbox. Dorothy *fills* the bill of a sister and the *caring* it takes to be one.

I write this rather lengthy description of Dorothy and *include* Bob because Bob passed away six years ago. I must tell you he was *unique* and believe me, one of a kind. With *respect and sadness* in losing him, it was the only funeral I attended that the University of Michigan fight song was played before saying our *last* good-byes. It was not just

91

about being an avid fan of U. of M., but because of *all* that he was, and the many ways he *touched* my life. Thanks, Dorothy—I *am* grateful that you decided to come to the wedding.

Thank you all for giving me your love, your time, your ear and your strength to carry me through some of the *deepest* valleys of my life.

I will not *forget* to *remember*—that you climbed the mountain of life with me, and for this, I remain *eternally grateful*.

Wouldn't you say I am *so lucky*? I bet your list is *longer* than you think if you just *begin* to contemplate the help *you* have been given, that really places others in the *sister category*.

I *honor* all of my sisters and shout from the rooftop—*Yeah—we're sisters*!

This writing of sisters has brought me to write the next chapter about the *acceptance* of one another. We remain sisters and friends by the *good* brought to our relationship, *by and through* each other. We come into each other's lives with our faults, and less than perfection. As we heal ourselves, we also are able to *help* in the healing of others. Let's remember—whatever *we* put into the *mix of life* determines whether it comes out good or bad. What power there is in *our* words and the *tremendous* impact of our actions on *each other*.

27

Acceptance—Don't Worry—It Won't Hurt

There are two ways of exerting one's strength: one is pushing down, the other is pulling up.
—Booker T. Washington

"*Acceptance* of each other creates happiness in our hearts and our souls." This statement may *stun* us, and we ask the question, "How could *this* be?" Accepting *everyone* will make us happy? "Hold on," we may say! "I don't *think* so."

If we look at it this way, we may be *more* convinced. Acceptance is not there to *pick* away at any of our *faults,* but to acknowledge *only* the *good* in each other. This is *not* saying that we have to *agree* with everything people do. We do not!

It only means we *may* have to *hunt* for a while, but everyone possesses *some trait of goodness*. We take the *quirks* of others, the *annoyances* of others, the *different* opinions of others and throw them in a *big* pot. Now, our *choice* is to reach in and pull their irritating ways and nuisances out of the pot, or look for *one good* quality in this person or persons. As we know, if we expect to meet the perfect person, our wait will be rather *lengthy*.

This brings us to the *intentions* of the heart, because this *is* where acceptance *really* starts. What are my *intentions* today? Are they filled with caring and goodness?

Let's look at the *gifts* we give to each other as our *precious jewels*. When we choose to *wear* them, we notice a *glimpse* from another. They have spotted the *glimmer* in us, obviously shown by our *display* of goodness. We can *trade* jewels with each other, if we wish. One day we may see a *precious jewel of knowledge,* we have given, being *worn* by another. On another day, we may notice a little more *patience,* another *shining* jewel. I *had* talked to this person about *practicing* a *little* more patience! They did *listen* to me, when they asked for my *advice.* What I am passing along seems to be helping them to *shine* a little brighter today! It is *creating* more happiness for them and others. I hear them *speak* and *my* words are on *their* tongue! This makes me *proud* to know that I had something of *value* to give.

Do I want to *show off* my jewels, or just keep them *hidden* in that safety deposit box—inside of me? Maybe, I'll just wear a *few* of my special adornments and save the *good* stuff for *myself* to enjoy. I hope others don't ask me if I have more, and find out—I'm not willing to share *all of me* with them.

> *Knowledge is Power*
> *Patience is finding something else to do, in the meantime.*
> *If you continually give, you will continually have.*
> —Chinese Proverb

This brings us to the *Don't Worry—It Won't Hurt* part of this chapter.

Practice *does* make Perfect. We are *practicing* acceptance. We will not *acquire* perfection, as no one does. We *just* want to cultivate a *desire* to be *loving* towards others.

I have this *theory* about accepting each other that does *not* inflict *pain* on us. My thinking is that the *soul* has *feelings.* The intentions of the *heart,* as to your performance every day, determines if the soul *stays* happy. I picture our *soul* being *down* in our body (I don't know why?) and of course, our *heart* on the upper torso.

I think this is what happens. The *intention of the heart* sends down your messages to the *soul.* Our soul then *relays* all of this *information,* and distributes our *intent* to all of our organs. This then creates our actions, behaviors, and feelings that we carry with us *inwardly* and our *outward display toward others.*

I haven't been able to *prove my theory yet but,* I'm still working on it!

I'm calling it H.S.H.M. We all love the *short* cuts in life, but I'll let you in on what these initials mean.

H is for *Honor*—first and last *throughout* our day
S is for *Simple*—*keeping* life that way
H is for *Holy*—remembering to place our *intentions* of the heart on this level
M is for *Mixture*—realizing this *daily* mixture can't fail us

In keeping with my theory, I believe we *can* accept everyone without much difficulty. I think you will *agree* that there doesn't *appear* to be any *worry* connected with this, and certainly you do not have to be *uncomfortable* by any type of *pain.* To live on this *level* of our being, our path becomes *strewn* with jewels that make *us* shine. This way of life *creates* a welcome of our efforts, by our soul. Boy, we don't even have to *polish* ourselves, like we *many times* must do with our *precious jewels,* but we sure do *sparkle* and *glisten,* when we *practice* acceptance.

28

I've Got New Blood

Create in me a clean heart, O God, and put a new and blessed spirit within me.

Have you ever had to have a blood transfusion? I did.

Two years ago I was given two pints of blood in the hospital because of hemorrhaging from my nose.

I was wondering whose blood I received? I sure was scared when a heard the doctor say, "It is time." "Two pints back to back and *quick*." I knew I was *sinking* into somewhere, but I couldn't speak. My nose was packed heavily in both nostrils and of course, that *can* hamper your speech, *even mine.* I was just amazed at how my body responded so quickly to someone else's blood.

I was wondering about the person who donated those *two* pints of blood? I guess it would be *two* people, not one. I do know this *new* blood helped my cholesterol count. My daughter said she thought that possibly the donors were vegetarians. Of course, I had eaten very little for about two weeks, and I have heard that IVs have *no fat content.*

So I'm thinking. Do you think that someone else's blood could make any changes in your body? *Like* make you a *better* person?

What if the man or woman were really a *good* person. I know they have to be *caring* about others, to give their blood in the first place.

I wonder if any of this is going to *rub off* on me? I guess blood doesn't really *rub off;* it sort of *mixes* around in your body. I wonder if their *good qualities* will come out in me?

Has there been any research on this subject? I find it pretty interesting. For example, these donors could be *more spiritual* than I. That would help *me* a great deal. I know they are *loving* because they took the time to *give* blood. I am *grateful* for those caring people. *It saved my life!*

I'm just going to *believe* that I did receive some *new* grace and *new* blessings from them. I hope others will notice the *difference* in me, because of my *new* blood.

29

Pay It Forward

I told them that the hand of my God had been gracious upon me, and also the words that the king had spoken to me. Then they said, "Let us start building!" So they committed themselves to the common good.

—Nehemiah 2:18

Have you seen the movie by chance called *Pay It Forward*? It sure was an enjoyable and heart-warming picture. It tells the story of a young boy who has an assignment in class to do *one* thing to *change* our world. He decides to try to help someone else that desperately needs his help. He is met with disappointment, but actually his idea is *passed* along and people begin to help each other. It is *not* in the plan, though, to try to reciprocate to the person who helped you, but to pass it on to help *someone else*. Therefore, *Pay It Forward*.

I was thinking about this idea in our everyday life. I have heard people speak about *never* having the chance to repay a debt owed. It could be their mother, father, relative, friend, or just someone who has done a special favor to help them out in *their* time of need. We may *lose* this person, before we are able to make our payment owed. We may *not* have been able to say *thank you* for whatever the reason. This seems to bring *sadness* to us and from what I have heard seems to *linger* in people's *hearts*.

There is *still* an opportunity for you to *pay back* what you feel is owed. It will just have to be to a *different* person. This is okay! I decided to start up this *new method* of payment. What do you think? You just *go ahead* and help someone who is in *need* and do it in *honor* of the *person* you feel has been short-changed by you, or you feel he/she didn't receive what was *due* them.

This is my *New Pay It Forward Strategy*!

Now, it doesn't matter if you *owe* money, time, possessions, or for that matter *what* the *debt* is. It only matters that in *paying back,* you *are* making restitution for what *you feel* you should have done for another. *Look around!* It won't be very difficult to *find* a need. It could be an elderly person, a child, a mother in crisis, or a family has fallen on hard times. It isn't important *who* it is or *what* you decide to do. *Feel* the peace. Isn't the *guilt* washing away? This happens when we *lift others up.*

Wow! I hope when I cross over to the other side, someone does this in *my* name, if they feel they didn't have a *chance* to *pay me back,* for whatever is bothering *them.* It would make me *so* happy that you decided to perform this task, *in my honor.* I will certainly be *listening* for *my* name!

Thanks for remembering me—*and oh*—by the way, the DEBT IS PAID.

Find a need and fill it—
Find a hurt and heal it!
                                    —Crystal Cathedral Calendar

In an outpouring of God's love, I give the most treasured gift
of all—my love to others.
                                    —*Daily Word*—Unity Village

30

What Is Written in "Your Book of Life"—Inside of You?

What we would write about ourselves is the facts, as we know them. It will consist of our journey here on earth, as we describe it. Each one's individual "Book" is—*their* walk, *their* path, *their* trip, and *their* way.

Our journey involves our experiences, what we have witnessed, and most importantly, the way we handled what we are dealt in life. The choices we make *create* the effect on our every decision of life.

But we'll simply *state* the facts, as *we* know them to be true. The problem lies in the *fact* that life is *not* simple! Sorrows, sadness, disappointments, loss and challenges are *never* easy. Although, we must remember, the days we are graced with happiness, love, joy, family and friendship. These are *gifts* given to us. Let's not forget to place those special treasures *in-between* the tough times. This keeps us positive and spurs our *willingness* to go on.

Our book about ourselves is *our* story. No one else can *copy* it. No *two* stories are *alike.* That's what makes us so *unique!*

> *When we open ourselves up to share the facts of our life, no one has the right to become the judge and the jury!* "Do unto others as if—you were the others."
>
> —Elbert Hubbard

How has your *walk* here on earth been? Were we sincere when we said, "I'll do better next time"? I think about my-

100

self, and what has happened to me. At times, I crawled. At times, I limped. At times, I had to pick myself up *off* the ground, *dust* myself off, and *carry* on. Those *baby* steps are *rough*. No wonder, when we watch those first steps our little ones take, their teetering back and forth, trying to hang on to something *solid*, becomes so understandable.

Wow! My book of life is *really* important! I didn't know it *holds* so much *power*, if only I *share* it? It has *lessons* for others to *learn*. Communicating about *my* life will help others to, hopefully, *not* make the same mistakes I have made. Maybe, some will even *heed* my advice?

Your *own* book is written in your head. It is *tucked* deep down in your heart and soul. *Share* it with others! *Talk* about what you *would* do, or *not* do again. We *learn* from each other. We are *all* teachers of life.

I just discovered something new! The book of *my* life is *SACRED*.

31

The End of the Line

The Lord is my shepherd, I shall not want.
He makes me lie down in green pastures;
He leads me beside still waters;
He restores my soul.

—Psalm 23:1–3

I had been on a retreat and this very gifted priest that day began to give a lesson on life. He took out a yardstick and asked us to measure how much of our life is left. Will your age fall at the beginning, the middle, or the end of the yardstick? This made a *profound* impact on me and sure made *me* begin to think. I decided instead of a yardstick, *I* would like to use a *tape rule*. At least the tape rule can *extend* my life—*if I pull on it—right?*

One day I was sitting at the railroad tracks waiting for a train to pass on by, and I got to thinking about that *yardstick* and the *short* amount of time we have here on earth. As I sat and waited, I began to compare my *life* to this train.

Let's pretend that every station is a *certain* time in our life, when the train makes a stop, may change tracks, picks up people or lets them off. That would mean that we could *decide* at any time whether *we* would *change* the course of our trip, take a different route, or just map out a *new* strategy for our life. All aboard! We step up on the train, hoping for a good trip to our *final* destination. We have to *realize* that the train is *not* stopping until we reach the next station. What we *do* at this *particular* station will be very important in *changing* the course of our trip, and our *life.* We *have* the power and the control *at this point,* rather than waiting until later. I'd better *hurry* if I have more to do! The train doesn't *stay* at any station too long. How *time* flies!

I do have certain plans for *my* life, but not just now.

I'll have time later.

I will expect that *I* will be able to complete *my* goals, without a problem.

I mapped out *my* trip and all of *my* life very carefully.

I will choose *my* life's track and the direction *I* will be comfortable with.

I know what *I* am doing?

Maybe—just—maybe, *I* should consider all of the choices *I* have made, and where they all fit into the whole picture *I* have painted?

I'll do that later, when *I* have more time to think about it.

I'm just too busy right now! It appears to *me* the road *I* chose is leading *me* down the right path.

Wow! There seems to be a bump on the tracks! The train feels a little *shaky* right now.

I hope *my* decisions for *my* life don't get bounced around!

I don't want everything *I* planned to change and get off track.

I hope this train doesn't jump the track.

This may set *me* in an entirely different direction.

I could even be detoured onto a whole other set of tracks, and pass up that station where *I* was going to make those changes, *I* was thinking about doing.

If this happens *I'll* have to question the choices, *I* have already made.

I might be forced to change!

I thought *my* life was on the right track, but now, with all of this turmoil going on, *I'm* not so sure!

I was contemplating changing some of *my* actions and behaviors later.

I thought *I* would do that when *I* arrived at the next station.

I guess *I* have procrastinated a bit, and now *I* am running out of time.

The Cars on the Train Are Roaring Fast Past All of the Stations!

I should have done more at that last station *I* visited.

I could have asked to stop there and get off to take care of *my* unfinished business of life.

It won't be long and *I'll* be at *my* final destination and the end of *my* earthly trip. *I* just realized *I* had waited and hoped that what is in store for *me* would turn out right, without much effort from *me*.

I was going to count all of the *I's, Me's,* and *My's* contained in this writing, up until this point. I thought it could be very discouraging for us to *realize* how much of this concerns just *one* person—in probably *two or more* people's lives. *This is the reason they are italicized* and most probably show a selfish side in many of the *choices* we make. Life is not just about *ME*. Life should be about *US*.

When I leave, I do want my earthly trip to be a place I am proud of and—others were proud to know me. I do want to be happy with myself for completing what I set out to do. I'd better *hurry* now, instead of *waiting* and stop *hoping* someone else *changes* things for me.

This was a most *difficult* chapter for me to write, and I didn't know why? When I began to compose this chapter, I had set out to make it a *short* one. My reasoning was that life *is* short! Yet, I couldn't seem to *get* the wording and my thoughts in some *semblance* of order. Then St. Anthony *nudged* me again one morning, during prayer time. I discovered the reason for all of this *disarray* in my head. *I was writing about myself.*

I was looking at my *own* life with *some* regrets. Oh, I kept *check* of those *many* blessings that I have received. I know the *gratitude* I feel for so much that has been given to *me* in my life.

It's *just* about those times that I *didn't* do what I thought I should.

It's *just* about those times wishing I had done *some* things differently.

It's *just* about those times I had the *opportunity* to display different reactions to situations, and I *muffed* it.

It's *just* about those times that I *didn't* say how much *I love you,* as *often* as I should have.

I'll *tell* myself and *believe* this *is* what I knew before a *greater* learning became a *part* of my life. I will say *I am sorry.* I will *ask forgiveness* for the many things I did *not* do, and the times that I *have failed.*

I have a chance *now* to make *good* choices and see them *through,* before I get to the end of the line. The *caboose* is coming! I can *see* it now way down on the tracks. Maybe, I could *pull* just *slightly* on that *tape rule* to give me a *little* more time here on earth; instead of using that *inflexible* yardstick. All of a sudden, I am *looking* at the Caboose! *Wow!*—That *is* the *end* of the train and the *end* of my earthly trip.

If I were to give my *own* eulogy, what will I speak about myself? I hope I would *not* have to say—

"There was so *much* more I wanted to *change* before I reached"

THE END OF THE LINE.

When we pray, God doesn't change things, he changes you for things.

Les Brown, one of the most lovable and caring motivational speakers, referred to our time of prayer and when we feel it is necessary to pray. He stated, "When there's a lot of shaking going on, I feel I'd better start praying." Then I realized—"It was God doing the shaking!"

"The Lord bless you and keep you; the Lord make his face to shine upon you, and be gracious to you; the Lord lift up his countenance upon you, and give you peace."

—Numbers 6:24–26

32

How Do We "Begin" Again?

Everyone thinks of changing the world, but no one thinks of changing himself.
—Leo Tolstoy

Expect to have hope rekindled. Expect your prayers to be answered in wondrous ways. The dry seasons in life do not last. The spring rains will come again.
—Sarah Ban Breathnach

The greatest use of life is to spend it for something that will outlast it.
—William James—Harvard Psychologist and Philosopher

After writing the previous chapter, reflecting on the end of our earthly trip, I thought about our *beginning*. This word, *beginning,* is filled with *hope*! I think it becomes *exciting,* as we examine *how* to accomplish this!

"To Begin Again"—is to *Start,* to *Come* into Being, to be *Reborn,* to be *New,* to be *First.* Do you get the feeling that this may be about changing *ourselves*? I wonder if that responsibility *cannot* wait on our procrastination?

This is our challenge—"To Begin." But just think about it! We don't have to *wait* for anyone or anything to give us *permission* "To Start." We can become a "New Person!" "Come into Being" also relays an even deeper meaning for us to contemplate. Coming into a *new* Being denotes change, and someone *different* emerges.

What *action will we take? What will we initiate?* What will be our new *course* of action? How will we *proceed*? How will our *performance* of life be different? Who will be our *source*, to help us make the change? What *kind* of "Being" do we *want* to "Come Into?"

<u>"To Begin"</u>

This means starting from somewhere!

This means we are able to become anew!

This means no set dates on our calendar!

This means no deadlines to be met!

This means no constraints!

This means time becomes a luxury!

This means no restrictions on what I can vow to do differently!

Have you heard the beautiful song written and sung by Dolly Parton? It is called "My Coat of Many Colors." It is the story of many different patches sewn together, to make a lovely covering, a *coat*, by her mother. It was the coat and *covering* she *wore* with *pride*. It was a "Labor of Love."

Actually, we can pick out our own *coat*, and *cover* ourselves in whatever way we choose to.

I *hope*—I choose something *attractive* to others.

I *hope*—I choose wanting to be *complimented* by others.

I *hope*—I choose to clothe myself in a *dress code* that will not become outdated.

I *hope*—I choose a classic coat so as *my style* remains popular.

"To Begin"—the patches will be the different individual experiences of my life. In putting all of these beautiful *pieces* together in a story order, we can tell of our learning and hopefully, our growing *into* the *"Being"* we want to become.

The more *worn-out* patches will go on top. I'll put them on my *shoulders*. My shoulders have carried much responsibility over the years. I will place the next pieces that are showing *wear*, on my *arms*. My arms have carried a heavy load many times. The middle front of my beautiful *coat* seems to be a little more *worn out*, as I have *rubbed* against more of the tough times of life. I am going to *sew* one of the *least* tattered and one of my *most* favorite patches, over my heart. I can't let my *patch* on my heart *wear* out! I don't want it to become *ragged* and be *left* hanging! Others will *really* notice! Oh, the more *weathered* patches may show a little, but that is *okay*. I tried to place all of the *least* worn patches in the *direction* of my heart, because this is where I do *all* the work.

My *patches* seem to be easier to *sew*, as I get to the bottom. I think that is because I have learned to place *stitches* where they really count. I will be really *careful* what I *fasten* to my life. I will *repair* what I can, and try to keep my life in *good* condition. I am going to try to *join* all of these *pieces* in the *sacred* order that they happened. I need to *restore* more good in my life, which has been *tattered* and *torn* from just *plain* living. I will take care of my *spiritual* and *special* covering, I wear every day! It is my experiences of life, my accomplishments, along with my mistakes, that have shaped *my* "Coat of Many Colors."

"To Come into Being," we *can* shed our *old* being and dress ourselves up in a much more *attractive* coat. My *intention* will be to look better on the *outside*, and *guard* the *good*, that I have learned on the *inside*. We have the *"Power to Change."* All that is required *is* the *desire*!

Life is *not* a dress rehearsal. There is not an *unlimited* amount of time to *change* our decision and *turn* in our *old* coat, for a *new* one! We are born into this world "*naked*." It is *our* choice as to what *covering* we will *wear*, throughout our life!

"*In the Beginning* was the Word and the Word was God—"

"To Begin"—"Start"—"Come into Being"—"Re-born"—"New"—"First."

When? *You decide.*

33

The Invisible Person Who Wrote My Book with Me
Lost and Found—Saint Anthony's Area of Expertise

I am God's treasure. God knows where I am at all times and keeps me safe.
—Daily Word—November 2000—Unity Village

I would like to tell you about the all-important person who wrote this book with me. His name is *ST. ANTHONY OF PADUA.*

He was born in Lisbon, Portugal, around the year 1195. His parents named him Fernando. At the age of fifteen, Fernando entered the order of St. Augustine with the hope of becoming an Augustinian priest. When he met five Franciscans from Coimbra on their way to Morocco, he was so taken by them and wished to serve the ministry of the conversion of those who did not know God. These friars soon met martyrdom and when their bones were returned to Lisbon and placed in the Augustinian Chapel, Fernando also wanted to die for Christ, as a martyr. He begged the superior of the Augustinian Monastery for permission to join the Franciscans. Reluctantly, the superior agreed and Fernando joined the Franciscans in the spring of 1220. He then changed his name to Anthony, in honor of St. Anthony of the Desert.

St. Anthony traveled and preached, but fell he ill with fever when he reached Africa. This fever remained with him for an entire year. Some historians think he had a combination of dropsy and asthma, or hepatitis. St. Anthony continued to travel despite his condition worsening. He wanted to die in Padua where he said God had worked so many wonders and conversions through his preaching to the poor. His lungs were filling with water and his breathing faint, when he opened his eyes and said, "I see God!" St. Anthony died on June 13, 1231. His tongue is *incorrupt* and is displayed at Basilica del Santo, in Padua.

Three months later the city of Padua sent the Pope records of forty-five miracles performed through Fr. Anthony's intercession. Those devoted to St. Anthony should ask favors of him only with *pure intention,* because this great saint is not *willing* to listen to those whose *aims* are not directed to their own spiritual growth and welfare. St. Anthony is one of the most popular saints of the Catholic Church.

Mine has been a strange story with Him. I actually had never prayed to Him except at those times when I had *lost* or misplaced something. I also know St. Anthony gives you *clues* to find what you are looking for. Some times it is in that *dark* corner where we *never* thought to look. *Check* again in that place that you *already* looked, if you feel the urge. This *is* the clue. St. Anthony will *truly* surprise you!

He has a really *big job* and seems *terribly* busy at times. That is why at times we have to *wait* for our items to be found. He may give us the *test* of patience and our *belief* in Him. He will come through for us, but we must remember to *Thank Him.* This *is* part of the *deal.*

I *did know* that St. Anthony was in *charge* of what we have lost, misplaced articles, can't remember, where are my car keys?—but, he has much more power than I realized. During my writings, I would just *hold* my medal of St. Anthony that I keep around my neck at all times, and asked to help me *find* those words for my new book. It feels sort of like getting a *hug.* This made me feel even *closer* to Him. I want to be sure I am relating my *deepest* feelings and experiences of life to others, in a helpful way. St. Anthony put *his words* on *my* paper many times. I am so *moved* by Him. I discovered that He also guides and leads us, when our *soul is lost!* He even gives *clues* to help you *find* a *path* to your soul. But you must listen *closely.*

I know today *why* St. Anthony came into my life. He is the patron saint of lost articles, which we would agree are *connected* to us, but he also takes care of what is *lost* that is *attached* to our *bodies.* I *didn't* know that, until I started writing my book. My breast was a *part* of me that I *lost* but not to be *recovered.* That is *okay*—because it *led* me to my soul. Sometimes we must *lose* something of value to find out what is really important. We may have *lost,* but what we have *found* is our serenity and the path to the real *importance* of life—*our soul.* St. Anthony will *point* you in the right direction if you just follow His *clues* to find a better way of life. He can't *steer* you wrong.

I entitled my book—"I *Lost* My Breast and *Found* My Soul," in honor of Him. I prayed to Him one day when I was contemplating a good title for my book. The title just *popped* into my head. I thought—that is a *great* title! I can *so honor* St. Anthony and hopefully, at the same time, relay what has happened to me since my mastectomy. *Thank You,* St. Anthony. I think You *picked* a pretty good title for what I *wanted* to say. Thanks for *sitting* beside me through all of these writings. I didn't know why at first, *I decided* to take Him on as my guiding light, and then I realized—*I didn't take Him on—He took me on.*

Saint Anthony is *truly* powerful. He will guide you to a place of *enlightenment* and *peace.* I extend to Him—the *greatest* honor and love.

I thank and praise *Him* for all he has done to help me. *Try* Him—*You'll like* Him.

SURE, I *LOST* MY BREAST—BUT I *FOUND* MY SOUL!